SALAD
~for~
DINNER

SALAD

~for~

DINNER

Complete Meals for All Seasons

JEANNE KELLEY

Photographs by Ryan Robert Miller

RIZZOLI
NEW YORK

New York Paris London Milan

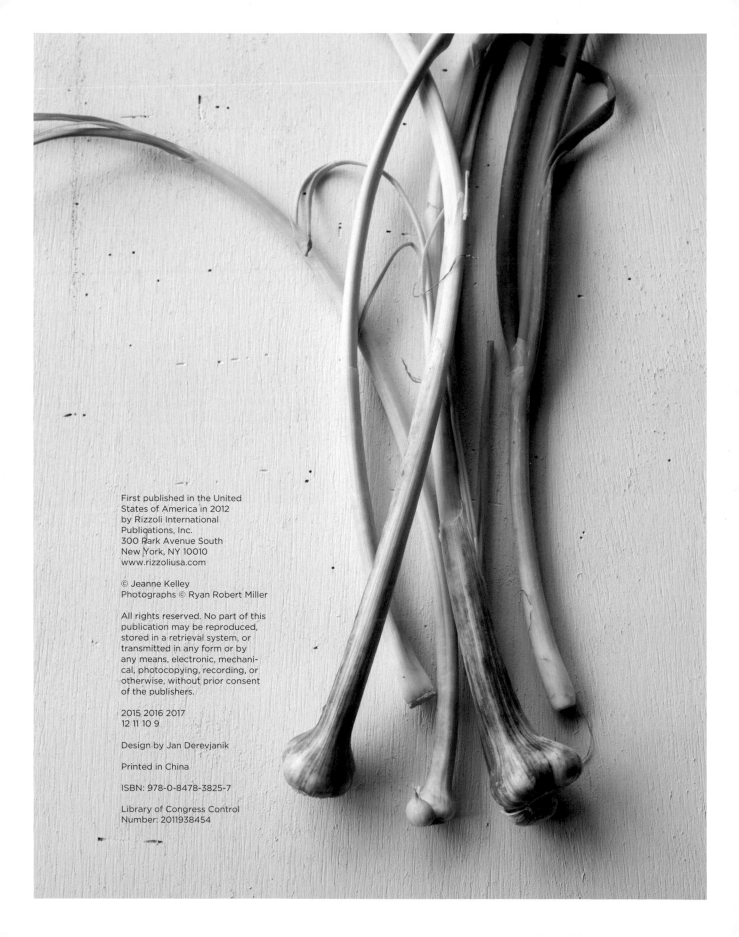

First published in the United
States of America in 2012
by Rizzoli International
Publications, Inc.
300 Park Avenue South
New York, NY 10010
www.rizzoliusa.com

© Jeanne Kelley
Photographs © Ryan Robert Miller

2015 2016 2017
12 11 10 9

Design by Jan Derevjanik

Printed in China

ISBN: 978-0-8478-3825-7

Library of Congress Control
Number: 2011938454

CONTENTS

A SALAD PRIMER..9

A Glossary of Greens 12

Foraging fo Salad 18

Washing and Storage..20

Growing Greens 24

The Salad Pantry..28

RECIPES

Vegetarian Salads...35

Salads with Fish and Seafood 81

Salads with Poultry 111

Salads with Meat..153

One Sweet Finish 199

INDEX...200

ACKNOWLEDGMENTS 208

CONVERSION CHART 208

OPPOSITE: Green garlic.

A SALAD PRIMER

A CELEBRATION OF CONTRASTS—COLOR, FLAVOR, AND TEXTURE—I CAN think of few more enticing things to eat than a carefully prepared salad. At home, I love to make and serve salads, and when dining out, I'm always on the lookout for inspired creations. In fact, salads are the first thing I look at on the menu at any restaurant. Salads can quickly clue you in to the quality of a kitchen, revealing the freshness and variety of ingredients used, and the ingenuity of the cook or chef. A good salad is exciting to eat, engaging the senses and awakening the palate. A salad can also be a meal in itself, and what a great way to eat. But salad for dinner? Most definitely. I include recipes that are well suited for lunch too, and a few even make great breakfasts.

Whether it's something sizzling off the grill paired with peppery greens, a mélange of chopped veggies and protein, or an artfully arranged *salade composée,* salad is so appealing—it's not only what we want to eat, but how we should eat. To be clear, I am not pushing "rabbit food." I enjoy steak, cured meats, rich cheeses, and crunchy, olive oil-infused croutons as much as I love arugula, tatsoi, romaine, watercress, and frisée. I just think that steak, cured meats, rich cheeses, and croutons taste *even better* when featured as part of a crisp, flavorful salad.

An added benefit is that eating this way can be nutritionally better for us. I am often asked how I manage to stay fit, given my job as a "food professional." This question, I'll admit, usually comes as I am proffering a slice of homemade frosted layer cake or indulging in a hefty wedge of still-warm-from-the-oven fruit pie. Like everybody, I am weight conscious, but I never diet. And while I exercise daily, I'm more of a stroller than a triathlete. So, with my healthy and enthusiastic appetite, why am I not as big as a house? I can only figure that salads are big part of the answer. *I really like vegetables* — especially in nutritious, well-balanced and delicious salads. But lest we're feeling a tad too virtuous, need I remind you that when you eat salad for dinner, there's almost always room for dessert?

Not every salad in this book features salad greens, but most do—after all, cool, crisp lettuce leaves are what most salads are all about. There are two schools of thought when it comes to salad greens. There is the slightly old-fashioned sense that the greens should be a neutral vehicle for salad dressings and goodies, and then there are folks like me, who really love and want to celebrate the freshness and flavor of the greens themselves. I like to spike my salad bowl with the wasabi-like punch of red mustard leaves, but I also appreciate the appropriate place for a tender, sweet leaf of folded Bibb.

Salad greens can be any number of leafy vegetables; mixtures can include not only lettuces, but spinach, kale, mustards, tender young chard, beet and pea leaves, and leafy herbs such as arugula, sorrel, and flat-leaf Italian parsley. In this book, recipes either feature specific greens or call for one of three blends: Baby Greens, Mixed Greens, or Peppery Greens.

BABY GREENS *are salad mixes of small, young leaves such as arugula, spinach, mizuna, baby red and green romaine, baby beet leaves, and baby frisée. Parsley leaves and fronds of tender chervil can be added, too. Mixed baby greens are often called mesclun.*

MIXED GREENS *are a combination of larger lettuces, such as red or green leaf, butter lettuce and* **romaine**, *and if you like it, some arugula.*

PEPPERY GREENS *are a blend of piquant greens such as arugula, frisée, curly endive, radicchio, red mustard, baby chard leaves,* **tatsoi,** *and mizuna. I might also add some spinach to this mix just so that it's not too peppery, and I list this in the ingredients.*

In a few of the recipes I call specifically for red greens, but only because I find the red color visually appealing; feel free to substitute "green" greens.

Keeping in mind that it's always optimal to use the freshest, best-quality greens available, when greens are plentiful, experiment with different combinations of lettuces, herbs, chicories, and mustards to personalize your own blends. Mixed Baby Greens just need to be small and tender, so if you luck out at the farmers' market and pick up a few perfect heads of Little Gem lettuce, by all means use Little Gem and only Little Gem. I really love Italian parsley and arugula. For Mixed Greens blend, I often use half arugula, half red romaine, and throw in a handful of parsley leaves for good measure. When it comes to Peppery Greens, one man's piquant is another's mild. Salads that call for peppery greens are robust, with bold dressings that stand up to the flavorful leaves. If a bowl of mustard greens is too much, consider using spinach leaves instead, spiked with a few spicier leaves of chicory or mustard. The important thing is to get a mix that works for your palate.

When cooking from this book, here are a few guidelines to keep in mind:

• *Read through the entire recipe to note any long chilling, marinating, and/or cooking times.*

• *Execute your* mise en place—*a French term which means to prepare each of the listed ingredients, chopping, blanching, etc.) before you begin to cook and/or assemble the dish. This is especially beneficial when it comes to prepping the greens—have them washed, dried, measured, and chilled before following through with the rest of the recipe.*

• *With the exception of a few recipes, salads taste best just after they are dressed, so make sure that everyone is at the table before tossing the salad.*

MESCLUN

Just what is mesclun? Spell-check doesn't recognize it. Every time I type it, I get a red line and prompt for mescaline, a hallucinogenic drug. "No," I groan back at the screen, "this is Doña Jeanne cooking, not Don Juan teaching, and what would the children think?" Of course mesclun is not derived from a rare desert cactus. It is simply a blend of young, tender salad greens. The name comes from a Provençal French dialect and means "mix." Whether the mix refers to a specific blend of a certain number of lettuces, herbs, mustards, and greens or to the simple act of blending is open to debate. However you grow, purchase, or combine your "mixed" salad, the mesclun should be tender, flavorful, and above all, fresh.

A Glossary of Greens

AMARANTH

Depending on your outlook, amaranth is either a weed or a boon. There are more than sixty varieties, in many shapes and sizes. The leaf color runs from pale green to red to dark purple. In India, Asia, and the Caribbean, amaranth is a popular cooking green. Here in the States you most commonly see it growing in gardens as an ornamental (in a tall, colorful form) or in the wild (in a less attractive form). Some varieties produce a tiny protein-packed grain. Red amaranth, used in small quantities, adds a flash of color and bite of nuttiness to salad green mixes.

ARUGULA

If I could pick only one salad green, it would have to be arugula. I love the bold, peppery flavor and the way it stands up to strong meats, cheeses, and sauces but does not overwhelm more delicately flavored vegetables, eggs, and pasta. There are several varieties of arugula, from giant, twelve-inch leaf varieties to tiny wild arugula with its pretty, deeply serrated leaves. Sometimes called rocket or *roquette*, arugula is technically a spring green, but it goes so well with robust summery flavors, especially those of the Mediterranean where it originated, that, luckily for us, it's available in markets year-round.

BABY BEET, PEA, AND FAVA BEAN LEAVES

Baby beet, pea, and fava bean leaves all make attractive and interesting additions to salads, but unless you garden, some of these greens might be hard to come by. If you purchase bunches of baby beets, there are often very small leaves at the center of the beet top. Clip, wash, and add these red-veined leaves to your salad mix. Pea tendrils are gaining in popularity and show up in the spring at farmers' markets and specialty food stores and are available year-round at Chinese markets. I prefer removing the pea-flavored leaves and discarding the wiry tendril. Fava leaves have a slight artichoke flavor; the plant grows like a weed, so consider planting a bean or two, if only for the leaves.

BUTTER LETTUCE

Butterhead, Bibb, Boston, and limestone are names for this delicate, mild-flavored lettuce. The tight, ruffled heads have velvety soft leaves and tender, butter-yellow folds in the center. There are countless varieties of butterhead lettuces to plant or source at farmers' markets, including red-tinged heirlooms such as Sierra. Butter lettuces are heat resistant and grow in the spring, summer, and fall. At the market, look for firm heads for the best value.

CABBAGE

Cabbage adds body and crunch to salads and slaws. If you use red cabbage, then you've got deep purple to add to your color palette. Cabbage is mild and sweet, but should be sliced very thinly as the leaves are tough.

CRISPHEAD LETTUCE

One lettuce that you won't find in any of the following recipes is iceberg. I don't like iceberg lettuce because it has no flavor. The "crisp head" gained popularity when the majority of Americans began buying lettuce in supermarkets as opposed to growing their own. The lettuce was cultivated because it transports so well. In order for iceberg to form its tight, crunchy, durable head, it must be blanched. Blanching is a horticultural technique used for growing plants such as cabbage and cauliflower in which the outer leaves are gathered and secured around the edible center of the crop, forcing it to grow into tight, compact heads. The process, because it keeps the sun at bay, also results in milder flavored vegetables—great for cabbage and cauliflower, not so good for lettuce. I know that some people appreciate iceberg for its crisp crunch factor, but it's too anemic for my taste.

BELGIAN ENDIVE

Belgian endive forms small, slender oval heads that are either white with a touch of chartreuse or burgundy at the leaf tip. This member of the common chicory family is forced, meaning that it does the majority of growing under sand to keep the heads from turning green, or red and leafing out. The narrow, spoonlike spears are best used as whole separated leaves, cut lengthwise into strips, or cut crosswise into rounds.

CURLY ENDIVE

Curly endive is a chicory like Belgian endive. Bitter, with dark green and very curly leaves, it is sometimes confused with frisée. Curly endive is larger, darker, and wider, with a more pronounced bitter flavor than frisée. Curly Endive is more common than frisée and usually available at markets. Use it to add depth to chopped salad mixes. It's also very good cooked.

ESCAROLE

Escarole is a mildly bitter chicory with broad, sturdy leaves that grow in flat rosettes. To be honest, it's not my favorite of the bitter greens for salads. I like it better cooked in pastas or wilted with lots of bacon for flavor. For a bit of bitter, I prefer delicate baby frisées or Belgian endive, the more robust curly endive or the more colorful radicchio.

FRISÉE

Frisée adds great flavor, texture, and color to salad mixes, but it is also wonderful when served on its own. Often marketed as "baby frisée" so as not to confuse it with curly endive (which is often mislabled as frisée), frisée is creamy yellow-white at the center and pale green at the leaf ends. Frisée has narrow leaves, about a half inch at the widest. When I don't have frisée growing in my garden, I find it at the farmers' market.

GREEN AND RED SALAD BOWL LETTUCE

These are the large, ruffled heads available at the supermarket. Sometimes simply labeled "red" or "green" leaf lettuce, this is the most popular of the loose-leaf variety of lettuce. Loose-leaf lettuces grow in a rosette shape. Great varieties to grow or search out at the farmers' market include Lollo Rossa, Cocarde, and deer tongue.

HERBS

Mild, leafy herbs such as Italian parsley, chervil, and sorrel make bold additions to salad blends. Herbs are best used in salad mixes where they won't compete with or overshadow the other ingredients in the salad. Salads that feature strong cheeses are great with herbs in the mix.

ITALIAN PARSLEY   SORREL

KALE

Kale is a popular green that is related to cabbage. There are many great varieties—Russian, curly, red, flowering or Lacinato kale (aka dinosaur kale or cavalo nero). Kale is usually eaten sautéed or stewed in soups or pastas, but an acid, such as lemon juice or vinegar, "cooks" kale the way vinaigrette can wilt a salad when it sits too long, resulting in a hearty and virtuous salad. Kale is robust enough that it can also be grilled.

LITTLE GEM LETTUCE

Salads made from *Lactuca sativa* have been popping up on the trendiest menus in last few years. This flavorful lettuce forms small, 5- to 6-inch heads with lightly ruffled, elongated leaves that in texture resemble a cross between romaine and butter lettuce. This cool-season lettuce tastes nutty and so sweet that the French name for it is *sucrine*, from *sucre,* or sugar.

MÂCHE

Mâche is a small, delicate salad green. With their vibrant grass-green color and subtle, nutty flavor, the tongue-shaped leaves and small rosettes make a pretty addition to baby salad mixes. Also called lamb's lettuce or corn salad, mâche is available at specialty foods stores.

MIZUNA

Mizuna is a Japanese mustard with feathery leaves and a spicy flavor. Mizuna is often used in stir-fries but tastes great raw, either on its own or as part of a peppery mix of greens. Mizuna is often included in purchased salad blends, but can be hard to find on its own. Look for it at Japanese markets or consider growing some.

OAKLEAF LETTUCE

Oakleaf lettuce is an heirloom loose-leaf variety. Oakleaf grows in red, green, and speckled rosette-shaped heads. The small heads feature a wide, crunchy center spine and tender lobes that are similar in shape to those of a white oak tree leaf.

PUNTARELLE

Puntarelle is a rare Roman chicory. In Italian, puntarelle trans-
lates as "little tips," a good description for the outer leaves on
the head of the chicory. The interior heart is thinly sliced, then
soaked in water, which softens the bitterness and causes the
shreds to curl. Prized for its bittersweet flavor, puntarelle is
available in the late fall and early winter. I don't call for this
exotic green in any of the following recipes (it's too hard to find),
but if you luck out and score some, both the leaves and the stalks would be wonderful in the
Roasted Beet and Blood Orange Salad (page 55) or as a garnish for the Frisée Salad with
Goat Cheese (page 75). As a side salad, toss it with the Anchovy Vinaigrette (page 95).

PURSLANE

Purslane is a salad herb with thick, teardrop-shaped leaves and a citrusy, tart, and succulent
taste. High in omega-3 fatty acids, purslane grows as a crop, ground cover (portulaca), and
weed. While it is sometimes available at Middle Eastern markets, you'll have a better chance
finding it at Mexican markets, where it is called *verdolaga*. Purslane is also available at farmers' markets in the summer months.

RADICCHIO

Radicchio is another member of the chicory family. For the radicchio to form a tight dark
purple head with the characteristic white veins, it must be either blanched (a process of
bundling and tying the outer leaves of the plant around the center) on the winter field or
aged in a dark, wet shed. Regardless of how it is cultivated, this colorful and deliciously bitter
salad green is available at most markets year-round.

RED MUSTARD

Bronze-leafed red mustard is another favorite of mine. I love the
color that the leaves add to salads as well as the strong Dijon-
mustard-meets-wasabi flavor. The large, tender leaves are good
cooked, wilted, and in small doses, raw. I grow red mustard by the
bundle, but it's often available at farmers' markets and specialty
foods stores. If you plan to eat the mustard raw, look for perky
leaves that are not wilted.

ROMAINE

Romaine or Cos lettuce has a characteristic thick spine and elongated leaves. This is a hardy lettuce that grows well in cool to cold weather. Romaine lettuce heads can get as large as 15 inches tall and come in green and red varieties. Red-speckled Rosalita and Rouge d'Hiver, with burgundy leaves, are particularly pretty types. When I want crunch in a salad, I use romaine—often chopped or sliced.

SWISS CHARD

Chard is a member of the beet family cultivated for the leaves instead of the root. Chard is generally cooked, but tiny baby leaves can be added to salad mixes and larger, still-tender leaves can be thinly sliced off the stalk and added to salad. Usually what's on offer at the store is too mature or too wilted for eating raw, so look for chard at the farmers' market. Chard is an excellent vegetable to plant. Available in so many colorful varieties (there's one called "rainbow") it can grow year-round and even in the snow.

SPINACH

While I'm not a huge fan of the bag-o-salad, I do very much like the packages of organic baby spinach that are all washed and ready to go. Because the small spinach leaves are thicker than most lettuces, they stay fresher on the journey from farm to bag to market to table. Baby spinach is great on its own or tossed into the salad mix. Mature spinach, however, will often get chalky in taste and squeak against the teeth, so it's best cooked.

TATSOI

Tatsoi, like mizuna, is another popular Asian salad green. The leaves are spoon shaped, hence it's sometimes called spoon cabbage. When small, tatsoi is sold as loose, two- to three-inch leaves. But it actually grows in a rosette, similar to baby bok choy and will sometimes be sold that way. It has a mild mustard-meets-cabbage flavor.

WATERCRESS

Cress is simply a leafy vegetable, and watercress is cress that grows in water. Some markets sell bunches of cut watercress and others vend a live, hydroponically grown type with a roots-in-foam appendage. The hydroponic variety is very mild. Watercress can also be foraged from clean brooks and ponds, and I highly recommend it—it's fresh, peppery—and free. Swaths of watercress appear every spring in the arroyo where I walk my dog. I am always tempted, but since the creek is mostly golf course runoff, I don't dare.

Foraging for Salad

THERE ARE MANY EDIBLES GROWING WILD IN OUR PARKS, FIELDS, AND FOR- ests that make interesting additions to salads. Commonly foraged plants include lamb's quarters, nettles, wood sorrel, and chickweed. Foraged greens can be added as curiosities and flavor punctuations to salad-greens blends. If you wanted to make a complete salad from foraged greens, you might channel your inner Rene Redzepi (the Noma Restaurant über chef and Nordic forager extraordinaire) to help you out with good flavor combinations. To do so, you'd imagine yourself as the animal that might eat the wild greens. Chickens love wood sorrel and dandelions, and the richness of a softly cooked egg yolk would nicely tame the foraged tart and bitter greens. And wouldn't a spicy grilled merguez sausage taste great atop a bed of lamb's quarters, drizzled with olive oil and spritzed with lemon?

When foraging, there are a few ground rules: Be sure to pick plants that have not been sprayed with pesticide or that grow near a contaminated water source. Don't forage too often in the same location, as overpicking can deplete the supply. Be respectful of surroundings and consider any wildlife that might need to eat the greens, too. Lastly, it's safest to consult an expert or botanist to make sure you don't dine on something nonedible.

CHICKWEED

Chickweed is a nutritious plant that grows abundantly in the spring. It dies back and turns brown quickly after blossoming, so it has a very short foraging season. Chickweed is high in minerals and vitamins, and it's pretty tasty, similar to mild watercress. The main drawback is that it is very similar in appearance to spurge—a poisonous weed.

DANDELION

As a kid, when I pondered the blossom of a dandelion, I figured the name was English. You know, a mash-up of "dandy" and "lion"— as the flowers looked like a snappy cartoon version of the maned king of cats. But the name is derived from the French *dents de lion,* because of the jagged-toothed appearance of the leaves. When  I lived in the southwest of France, I learned another name for the weed that we would forage for in the countryside. *Le pis-en-lit,* so named because of the green's diuretic qualities, is popular served with a warm bacon vinaigrette. Despite enjoying the salad, I luckily did not wet the bed. Foraged dandelion greens, when picked very small, add a pleasant bitterness to a Peppery Greens mix. Commercially grown dandelion greens tend to be very bitter and should be added to salad blends with caution.

LAMB'S QUARTERS

Lamb's quarters have a nutty, floury flavor. The leaves are good in a salad mix, but the stems are edible, too. Lamb's quarters are ubiquitous. They can be foraged from spring until fall in fields, vacant lots, gardens, and parks.

MINER'S LETTUCE

Miner's lettuce has tender, round, lily-pad-shaped leaves and a mildly tart flavor. The annual is wild and unique to the West. It grows as far north as Alaska and as far south as Central America, but is most abundant in California. Miners who flocked west during the gold rush ate the lettuce to ward off scurvy (it's a good source of vitamin C)—hence the moniker. You can find stands of the plant in shady upland areas in spring and early summer. Once picked, it should be eaten quickly. I don't call for miner's lettuce in any of my salads because it hardly seems fair to list a green that requires foraging, and only on the Left Coast, but if it happens to grow wild in your locale, by all means, add it to the mix, as it's a rare treat.

NETTLES

Nettles grow, much to hikers' chagrin, along wood and forest trails in the spring in areas where the rainfall is heavy. Because they sting, nettles are tricky to harvest. Wear gloves to pick the young, tender leaves. Soak the leaves in cold water for at least an hour to remove the chemicals that zing. Enjoy their vitamin-rich and delicate spinach flavor in spring salad blends.

WOOD SORREL

Wood sorrel is the bane of many gardens. The prolific weed, known as oxalis, has a complex root system, making it difficult to eradicate. So, as a gardener, if you can't beat it, why not eat it? As a child, I nibbled on stalks of wood sorrel while running wild with pals on undeveloped hillsides. We called it sour grass, and it is indeed sour. A few lobes of the shamrock-shaped leaves make a tart addition to salads, but the key word here is "few."

Washing and Storage

LETTUCES AND SALAD GREENS SHOULD BE WASHED CAREFULLY. A GUSH OF water from the faucet can bruise most greens so it's best to give your salad a bath instead of a shower. Fill the sink or a large bowl with cold water and swish individual leaves or heads of lettuce gently in the water. Allow the greens to bathe in the water just long enough to loosen the dirt on the leaves. You can use a salad spinner for this, making it easy to lift the greens in the basket out of the water for drainage. A side benefit to this cleaning process is that the greens will absorb water into their cells, rehydrating to become plumper and crisper. Just don't let the greens sit in the water for too long, or they will become dark and waterlogged. I recycle the dirty "bath" water to water the potted plants on my terrace.

After washing, dry the greens carefully. A salad spinner makes quick work of this task. Spin the greens gently, then pour out the water that drains to the bottom of the spinner and whirl the greens again. If you don't have a spinner, layer the greens between clean, absorbent dish towels and gently pat dry.

Store the greens in the refrigerator in a resealable plastic container lined with a small dish towel or in resealable plastic bags. You can also store salad greens in the salad spinner to crisp effect. Leave as little space as possible in the storage container, and if you are using plastic bags, squeeze out as much air as you can before sealing. Salad greens are still respirating, so any oxygen they breathe in will be exhaled as carbon dioxide, which will cause them to wilt.

Farmers' market greens will keep about one week. Greens picked from the garden will keep slightly longer. Supermarket greens prepped in bags or boxes have "sell by" dates, but for best taste should be used a few days before. Head lettuces from the supermarket will keep for about four days.

SALAD SPINNER

You don't really need any specialty cooking equipment to make a good salad. The only exception to this gadget-free dish is the salad spinner. This handy tool quickly and gently removes excess moisture from even the tenderest greens. I remember the days of layering lettuce leaves to dry on thin cotton dish towels. It was such a chore, and often our salads were bruised. Some folks turn to paper towels, but they really don't do the trick either. With a good salad spinner, you can both efficiently wash and dry the salad greens. The large drum-shaped tool can be a storage problem, but several models are also designed to keep greens crisp in the refrigerator, which is

Washing tatsoi (front) and red mustard with arugula (rear).

Snap peas, pea tendrils, and pea blossoms.

where you will usually find mine—filled with freshly picked and washed salad greens, ready to go. Some other items that are helpful to have on hand: an electric blender for pureed dressings; large, shallow bowls; a large, wide measuring bowl; salad servers, and a small whisk for blending dressings.

MEASURING GREENS

Measuring salad greens is tricky. I call for cups in the following recipes, but I don't really intend for you pack delicate greens into a 1- or 2-cup measuring cup, which could bruise them. I considered calling for a number of heads, but not all greens grow as heads, and size varies greatly. I like the precision of weight measurements, but here again I was stymied when it comes to measuring mixes of different greens. Six cups of arugula and frisée weigh 4½ ounces, but the same amount of romaine cut into bite-size pieces weighs in at a whopping 8½ ounces. Also, not everyone owns a scale. So, for the purposes of this book, I've found that the best way to measure the greens is in a large, shallow 8-cup measuring bowl. I'd like to instruct you to "loosely pack" them, but those terms are contradictory, so very gently compress the greens when measuring.

EATING SEASONALLY

When most of us think of salad as a meal, we think of warm summer nights and "no-cook" dinners culled from the fridge or the garden. But salad makes a satisfying repast year-round. Warm salads such as the Red Mustard and Bread Salad with Roast Chicken (page 120) and the Wilted Swiss Chard Salad with Caramelized Onions, Croutons, and Fried Eggs (page 70) are excellent choices for chilly winter or fall nights. Ingredients like peas and asparagus are lovely in salads that celebrate spring, and indeed summer is the season of many salad favorites such as tomatoes, cucumbers, and corn. We know that fruits and vegetables taste best when they are as freshly picked and locally grown as possible, but with the giant supermarkets carrying so much produce year-round, it's not always clear which fruits and vegetables are "in season."

The following chart is a simple guideline highlighting some of the seasonal ingredients featured in these salads. The list is only partial, as many ingredients are actually good year-round. That Chicken, Avocado, and Mango Salad (page 140)? It will work just as well on a summer night as it will for lunch on a winter's day.

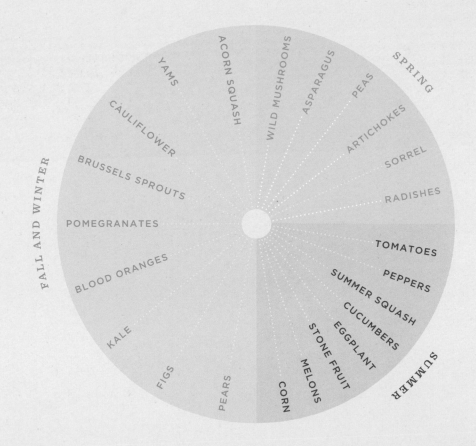

GREENS TO GO

If you pack a salad to take to work for lunch, not only are you giving yourself a midday meal to look forward to, but a salad from home is also good for your health and your pocketbook. A salad for an evening picnic is brilliant in that it's supposed to be served cold. Salads that can be prepared a day ahead (see page 26 for list) make it easy—just spoon the mix into a Tupper and go. Green salads, however, require a little more finesse to stay perky and appetizing when going from home to work or play. I've packed salads to-go a variety of ways and the following have worked the best for me.

• **For individual servings,** start with shallow rectangular plastic containers with tight-fitting lids. The tightly fitting lid is super important—you don't want the dressing to leak out all over your picnic basket or briefcase. You can combine the salad and dressing in one container if you pack them like this: Pour a single serving of dressing into the bottom of a wide food container large enough to accommodate a serving of salad. You can use a bowl or flat, box shape; just make sure it's easy to toss and eat the salad from it. First, layer any fruits or vegetables that can marinate (such as apples or tomatoes) directly over the dressing. Add the remaining components, placing any items you'd like to stay crisp on top. (The Greek Salad works really well packed this way.) When you're ready to eat the salad, toss gently with your fork and enjoy.

• Use a Japanese bento box. Bento boxes are ingeniously designed for transporting a meal with all the components packed neat and tidy in separate little resealable compartments. With a bento box, the greens, fruit, cheese, nuts, and dressing all stay fresh and beautiful until ultimately being combined (in the main compartment). Look for bento boxes in Japanese markets or online.

• **For a crowd,** consider packing various chopped and prepped ingredients separately into resealable plastic bags (kindly consider the eco kind). Make the dressing in a jar and arrange the jar and bags in a large bowl for transport. If your pals bring their own forks and plates, all you will return home with is an empty bowl. Bring a tall kitchen trash bag to make it easy.

Growing Greens

FOR A GOOD VARIETY OF FLAVORFUL GREENS, SHOP AT FARMERS' MARKETS or look into having fresh lettuces delivered from a CSA (Community Supported Agriculture) farm in your area. CSAs are a convenient way to purchase seasonal, local produce directly from the farmer. Typically, one buys "shares" in an upcoming harvest from a farm, and a weekly selection of produce is delivered to your home or to a central pick-up location, such as a natural foods store. With most CSAs, you won't necessarily know in advance which vegetables you might receive each week, and there is sometimes an element of shared risk involved, but they are an excellent way to support farmers and procure local produce crops. To get information about CSAs, look to your local natural foods store or co-ops or to one of the many Web sites set up to help you find area farmers involved in the program. (A good place to start is Localharvest.org)

Conveniently, many supermarkets these days carry a vast selection of salad greens. At the decidedly not fancy megamarket in my neighborhood, I can usually find all the usual suspects—romaine, red leaf, green leaf, and frisée, along with radicchio and still-growing watercress and butter lettuce.

But for the best taste, variety, availability, and even affordability, consider growing your own. Lettuces and salad greens are some of the easiest vegetables to grow, and arugula, my

Baby cabbage.

Romaine rouge d' hiver in recycled wood planter.

favorite, grows like a weed. Propagating salad greens need not require big investments of time, money, and space. A two-dollar packet of mesclun mix, mixed baby lettuces scattered into a pot filled with a portion of ten-bucks-a-bag potting soil will yield a couple of seasons' or even years' worth of greens. A raised bed in a backyard or community garden is an ideal place for planting lettuce. The 5x10-foot bed in my community garden keeps me in greens year-round. If you live in an apartment, a vegetable-planting device such as a Grow Box situated on a sunny patio or balcony would work. My husband, Martin, and I have even fashioned a planter out of a nursery flat and recycled lumber. A nursery flat is a 16x16x2-inch plastic planter with a perforated bottom for good drainage. Bordered with 4- to 8-inch-wide pieces of wood, the flats become deep enough for long-term growing and good, moist soil. The transportable boxes are handy in that they can moved in and out of the sun, or in and out of the cold, depending on the climate.

I love strongly flavored, piquant greens, which happens to suit my growing climate well. In sunny Southern California, lettuces tend to bolt (go to seed) quickly, so I search out bolt-resistant varieties to plant. To discover varieties of lettuce and salad greens suitable for your planting zone, consider talking to your local independent nurseryman or consult an area "Master Gardener". Master Gardeners are garden enthusiasts who get horticultural and community outreach training through a network of university extension programs—one is usually a quick internet-search away.

Generally, lettuces should be planted in early spring for spring, summer, and fall harvesting in snowy climates. Where winters are mild, fall is the best time to plant salad greens for use all winter and into spring, when it's time to plant heat-resistant varieties to enjoy in the summer. As I especially love arugula, I plant it successively in order to enjoy it in salads all year long.

A few tips for growing great greens:

- *In climates where winter freezes, situate your planter in full sun; where winters are mild, place it in partial shade.*

- *Sow seeds in rich, well-draining soil that is neither too sandy or clay-like.*

- *Thin seedlings to within an inch or two for mesclun mix and up to six inches apart for arugula, spinach, and head-forming varieties of lettuce.*

- *Water gently and regularly.*

- *Harvest greens regularly to enjoy them at their peak and to encourage new growth.*

MAKE-AHEAD SALADS

A few salads in the book can be prepared in advance and several can be made almost completely ahead and require just a little last-minute preparation. These could be great options for office lunches, picnics, or potlucks.

DAY-AHEAD SALADS

Moroccan-Spiced Roasted Cauliflower and Carrot Salad with Chickpeas and Couscous, *page 44*

Toasted Barley, Long Bean, and Shiitake Mushroom Salad with Teriyaki Tofu , *page 46*

Freekeh Salad with Apricots, Grilled Halloumi, and Zucchini, *page 78*

Baby Octopus and White Bean Salad, *page 98*

Paella Salad, *page 108*

SALADS MOSTLY MADE AHEAD WITH A LITTLE LAST-MINUTE FINISHING

Mexican Beach Ceviche with Avocado, page105

Seafood-Stuffed Avocado Salad, *page 100*

Curried Chicken on Baby Spinach with Mango Chutney Dressing and Garlic Naan Crisps, *page 117*

Indonesian Slaw with Pineapple, Chicken, and Spicy Peanut Dressing, *page 116*

Chinese-Style Chicken Salad with Tangerines, *page 114*

Summertime Corn and Ham Salad, *page 164*

Trio of Grated Salads with Hearty Greens and Pan-Seared Sausages, *page 198*

Kale Salad with Wheat Berries, Parmesan, Pine Nuts and Currants, *page 43*

THE SALAD TIMELINE

Many of the salads in this book come together quickly—a little spin, chop, dress, and toss and you've got a meal. Yet, in order to create varied and sophisticated salads, I can't deny that some of the recipes require a little more work dicing, mincing, whisking, grilling, or simmering. You can keep things running smoothly and relatively effortlessly in the kitchen by doing a bit of menu planning. By making some of the components of the salads earlier in the day or week, actual cooking at mealtime is not so hectic.

1 WEEK AHEAD→	4 DAYS AHEAD→	3 DAYS TO 1 DAY AHEAD→
Roast and chill beets, boil and chill eggs, glaze nuts.	Wash, dry, and refrigerate—do not chop or tear—salad greens.	Prepare vinaigrettes, dressings, and sauces.

HOLD THE LETTUCE

In some parts of the country, there are times of the year when lettuce is not locally available, or what is at the market is wilted, pale, and sad. But you can make a great salad without lettuce. Cabbage, parsley, kale, Brussels sprouts, and chard all make great salad greens. Other salads, like grain and pasta salads, rely on chopped fruit, herbs, and vegetables for freshness and crunch.

Moroccan-Spiced Roasted Cauliflower and Carrot Salad with Chickpeas and Couscous, *page 44*

Roasted Acorn Squash and Brussels Sprout Salad with Quinoa, Pepitas, and Pomegranates, *page 41*

Toasted Barley, Long Bean, and Shiitake Mushroom Salad with Teriyaki Tofu, *page 46*

Pea and Orecchiette Salad with Perlini Mozzarella and Mint, *page 63*

Kohlrabi and Black Quinoa Salad with Coconut and Cashews, *page 61*

Wilted Swiss Chard Salad with Caramelized Onions, Croutons, and Fried Eggs, *page 70*

Kale Salad with Wheat Berries, Parmesan, Pine Nuts and Currants, *page 43*

Freekeh Salad with Apricots, Grilled Halloumi, and Zucchini, *page 78*

Singapore-Style Chinese New Year Raw Fish "Tossed" Salad, *page 89*

White Anchovy, Potato, and Parsley Salad, *page 91*

Baby Octopus and White Bean Salad, *page 98*

Paella Salad, *page 108*

Indonesian Slaw with Pineapple, Chicken, and Spicy Peanut Dressing, *page 116*

Red Mustard and Bread Salad with Roast Chicken, *page 120*

Jeanne's Jar Chopped Salad, *page 125*

Kale and Cornbread Salad, *page 157*

Grilled Kale with Lamb and Garlic-Mint Yogurt Dressing, *page 197*

Buckwheat Soba Noodles with Sesame Dressing, Tofu, and Asian Greens, *page 60*

Chinese-Style Chicken Salad with Tangerines, *page 114*

2 DAYS AHEAD→	1 DAY AHEAD→	6 HOURS AHEAD→	4 HOURS AHEAD→	2 HOURS AHEAD→	1 HOUR AHEAD
Boil and refrigerate cooked vegetable additions to salads such as asparagus, haricots verts, and yams.	Marinate meats Chop or slice durable vegetables such as celery and bell pepper.	Marinate chicken.	Crumble, grate, slice, dice, or shave cheese.	Tear or chop salad greens.	Assemble green salads. Cover and chill until ready to dress and serve.
Roast, marinate, or salt chicken.	Fry tortilla and wonton strips.				
Cook and chill grains such as farro and barley.					
Bake croutons, crostini, crisps, chips, cornbread, and toasts.					

The Salad Pantry

VINAIGRETTES AND DRESSINGS ARE THE SAUCES OF SALAD. A COMBINATION of fat, acid, and flavor, they're what make a salad a pleasure to eat, rather than a penance. Fats include oil, cream, mayonnaise, yogurt, and sour cream. Acid is vinegar or citrus juice. Flavors are an infinite combination of alliums, herbs, and spices. Fat mellows the acid, and acid brightens all the flavors. The fat also acts as a vector for aromatic spices, while the acid intensifies herbal flavors. Seasoned with salt, the result is a simply executed yet balanced sauce that can make a bowl of lettuce taste complexly delightful.

The standard ratio for vinaigrette is three parts oil to one part vinegar, but this can vary depending on the acidity of the vinegar and other components added to the vinaigrette. Some vinaigrettes form a creamy emulsion—an emulsion being a smooth blend of liquid fat and a waterlike fluid. Additions that help to emulsify vinaigrettes are egg yolks and milk-based proteins. Finely powdered or granular mixtures such as mustard, tahini, and peanut butter act as stabilizers and also help to keep a vinaigrette creamy in appearance. An opaque, homogenous blend can be attractive drizzled over greens, but so too is a bowl of green-gold fruity olive oil with suspended gems of vinegar that get whisked to blend just before tossing.

NUTS

Chopped nuts are such an important element to so many salads. Nuts add flavor, crunch, and high-satiety healthy fats and protein. Studies show that people who eat diets rich in nuts tend to stay lean. To bring out the most flavor and bite, nuts should be roasted or toasted. When it comes to cashews or pistachios, store-bought roasted nuts are the best choice. Walnuts, pecans, and almonds taste freshest when purchased raw and toasted just before using. To toast nuts, spread them out in a single layer and cook them in a preheated 375°F oven until they are fragrant and beginning to darken slightly in color, about 8 to 10 minutes for pecans and walnuts and 10 to 12 minutes for almonds.

OILS

For the same reason I take a pass on iceberg lettuce, you won't find vegetable oil in any of the vinaigrettes or salad dressings in this book. I want my salads to be flavorful—so why just add a neutral oil that will only blunt the acid of vinegar or lemon juice when I can add taste at the same time? Fruity extra-virgin olive oil, toasted nut oils, sesame oil—all these flavorfully enhance the salads without dulling flavor.

Grains and legumes (clockwise from top): wild rice, barley, yellow and black quinoa, French lentils, brown rice, farro.

Dressings (clockwise from top): lime-ancho vinaigrette, mustard-shallot vinaigrette, creamy blue cheese dressing, creamy lime avocado dressing, black olive vinaigrette, pesto vinaigrette.

SALT

Salt—or salty-flavored things such as soy sauce, fish sauce, or anchovies—is an important factor in salads, vinaigrettes, and dressings. Commercially available bottled salad dressings are loaded with sodium. Making your own dressings allows you to control the amount of salt. I call for exact amounts in most of my dressings in order to get the balance just right. If you don't like salt, or are on a sodium-restricted diet, you may want to add salt to taste and ignore my measures. For seasoning salads as well as meats, in salad dressings, and to salt boiling water, I use kosher salt. When I want to add a touch to finish a salad, in particular the greens, some sliced vegetables, or a cooked egg, I choose flakes of good-quality sea salt.

VINEGAR

I have several varieties of vinegar in my cupboard—red wine vinegar, white wine vinegar, organic unfiltered cider vinegar, sherry vinegar, balsamic, white balsamic, and rice wine vinegar. The flavor, quality, and acidity of vinegar vary greatly, and it pays to shop around. Good balsamic is everywhere, while white wine and sherry vinegar have gotten a little harder to find (I purchase them at a French import store). When it comes to red wine vinegar, it's worth it to source a good oak-aged variety as oak aging will add hints of vanilla and spice.

DRESSING APPROPRIATELY

"Toss the salad with enough dressing to coat and season to taste." You'll see that instruction throughout this book—and just what does that mean? Vinaigrettes and dressings season greens, and they also coat them; some folks like a generous dousing, while others, like me, prefer a lightly dressed salad. Many of the salads instruct to toss the salads with a measured amount, then pass extra vinaigrette or dressing with the salad, allowing people to "season" their salads to their own taste. When crafting your own salads, it's handy to know which dressings or vinaigrettes are best suited to the myriad greens you might toss into the bowl. In general, strong, assertive dressings go well with robust, peppery greens. Salty additions to dressings, such as bacon bits, olives, and anchovies complement bitter, crisp, and succulent greens. Super creamy or thick dressings need a lettuce with some body to hold up to the weight of the dressing. Sweet touches of honey, maple, or mango chutney bring out the best in spinach and serve to mellow peppery greens. Here are some good matchups of greens and dressings.

BABY GREENS

Blood Orange-Sherry Vinaigrette, *page 55*
Lemon Vinaigrette, *page 85*
Mustard-Shallot Vinaigrette, *page 145*
Five-Spice Vinaigrette, *page 150*
Quince Vinaigrette, *page 161*
Sherry Vinaigrette, *page 184*

ROMAINE

Creamy Lime-Avocado Dressing, *page 49*
Oregano Vinaigrette, *page 52*
Green Goddess Dressing, *page 66*
Pesto Vinaigrette, *page 71*
Anchovy Vinaigrette, *page 95*
Horseradish Cream, *page 99*
Creamy Blue Cheese Dressing, *page 135*
Quince Vinaigrette, *page 161*
Mediterranean Lemon Dressing, *page 196*

MIXED GREENS

Lime-Ancho Vinaigrette, *page 39*
Oregano Vinaigrette, *page 52*
Blood Orange–Sherry Vinaigrette, *page 55*
Sesame Dressing, *page 60*
Mediterranean Lemon Dressing, *page 105*
Spicy Peanut Dressing, *page 116*
Mango Chutney Dressing, *page 117*
Creamy Blue Cheese Dressing, *page 135*
Thai Dressing, *page 139*
Mustard-Shallot Vinaigrette, *page 145*
Sherry Vinaigrette, *page 184*
Honey-Marjoram Vinaigrette, *page 187*

BUTTER LETTUCE

Creamy Lime-Avocado Dressing, *page 49*
Green Goddess Dressing, *page 66*
Lemon Vinaigrette, *page 85*

BITTER GREENS

Moroccan-Spiced Dressing, *page 45*
Black Olive Vinaigrette, *page 67*
Anchovy Vinaigrette, *page 95*
Five-Spice Vinaigrette, *page 150*

KALE AND CABBAGE

Moroccan-Spiced Dressing, *page 45*
Spicy Peanut Dressing, *page 116*
Thai Dressing, *page 139*
Chimichurri Vinaigrette, *page 176*
Garlic-Mint Yogurt Dressing, *page 197*

ARUGULA

Pesto Vinaigrette, *page 71*
Sherry Vinaigrette, *page 184*
Mediterranean Lemon Dressing, *page 196*

SPINACH

Sesame Dressing, *page 60*
Pesto Vinaigrette, *page 71*
Spicy Peanut Dressing, *page 116*
Mango Chutney Dressing, *page 117*
Maple-Bacon Vinaigrette, *page 129*
Mediterranean Lemon Dressing, *page 196*
Garlic-Mint Yogurt Dressing, *page 197*

PEPPERY GREENS

Black Olive Vinaigrette, *page 67*
Anchovy Vinaigrette, *page 95*
Horseradish Cream, *page 99*
Maple-Bacon Vinaigrette, *page 129*
Creamy Blue Cheese Dressing, *page 135*
Quince Vinaigrette, *page 161*
Chimichurri Vinaigrette, *page 176*
Honey-Marjoram Vinaigrette, *page 187*

MIX AND MATCH

Over the course of a month, my refrigerator gets cluttered with random jars of vinaigrettes and dressings, each containing about two tablespoons of orphaned sauce. They all took precious time to prepare and are made with quality ingredients and love, so I wouldn't dream of tossing them. Sometimes the dressings come in handy when mixing up a small salad for a quick solo lunch or dinner, but more often than not, they languish. So what's to be done when the condiment count is out of control?

Many of the vinaigrettes and dressings can be combined for use as a dressing on a mixed green salad. Vinaigrettes with the same acid, i.e., lemon juice or vinegar, combine well. The Quince Vinaigrette, made with sherry wine vinegar, becomes more tart and complex when blended with the Blood Orange–Sherry Vinaigrette or the Sherry Vinaigrette. It's a good idea to label leftover dressings so you don't forget what they're made of and accidentally pair Black Olive with Sesame or Anchovy with Five-Spice. When mixing and matching, keep flavor profiles similar or complementary. Italian-style vinaigrettes such as Black Olive, Oregano, and Anchovy taste great all tossed together with peppery greens or potato salad.

THE VERSATILE VINAIGRETTE

Celebrity chef Tom Colicchio considers vinaigrette the most underappreciated sauce in existence. Well, I think vinaigrettes are mostly well appreciated on salads—it's just elsewhere in the kitchen that their delicate balance of acid, fat, and flavor is underutilized. The following chart suggests other creative ways to use them, in case you have leftovers or want to make a double batch.

SAUCES FOR GRILLED MEAT OR POULTRY

Blood Orange-Sherry Vinaigrette, *page 55*
Pesto Vinaigrette, *page 71*
Chimichurri Vinaigrette, *page 176*

SAUCES FOR FISH

Lime-Ancho Vinaigrette, *page 39*
Green Goddess Dressing, *page 66*
Black Olive Vinaigrette, *page 67*
Pesto Vinaigrette, *page 71*
Mediterranean Lemon Dressing, *page 196*

SAUCES ON GRILLED OR STEAMED VEGETABLES

Moroccan-Spiced Dressing, *page 45*
Sesame Dressing, *page 60*
Lemon Vinaigrette, *page 85*
Five-Spice Vinaigrette, *page 150*

SAUCES ON SAUTÉED SPINACH, CHARD, OR KALE

Sesame Dressing, *page 60*
Black Olive Vinaigrette, *page 67*
Maple-Bacon Vinaigrette, *page 129*

AS SANDWICH SPREADS

Pesto Vinaigrette, *page 71* • *Try it with tomato and fresh mozzarella subs.*
Horseradish Cream, *page 99* • *Try it with roast beef or turkey or smoked fish with watercress on rye bread.*
Quince Vinaigrette, *page 161* • *Try it with Serrano ham or chorizo with Manchego cheese on rustic bread buns.*
Chimichurri Vinaigrette, *page 176* • *Try it with leftover thinly sliced beef or lamb with roasted peppers on sourdough bread.*

AS DIPS FOR CRUDITÉS AND CHIPS

Creamy Lime-Avocado Dressing, *page 49*
Creamy Blue Cheese Dressing, *page 135*
Garlic-Mint Yogurt Dressing, *page 197*

GOOD MARINADES

Lime-Ancho Vinaigrette, *page 39* • *chicken and seafood*
Oregano Vinaigrette, *page 52* • *multipurpose*
Black Olive Vinaigrette, *page 67* • *multipurpose*
Anchovy Vinaigrette, *page 95* • *lamb, salmon*
Mango Chutney Dressing, *page 117* • *chicken and pork*
Thai Dressing, *page 139* • *multipurpose*
Five-Spice Vinaigrette, *page 150* • *beef, pork, duck*
Mediterranean Lemon Dressing, *page 196* • *seafood and chicken*

GREAT NOODLE OR PASTA SAUCES

Sesame Dressing, *page 60*
Pesto Vinaigrette, *page 71*
Spicy Peanut Dressing, *page 116*
Lemon-Chive Drizzle, *page 165*

SALAD CODE

A friend of mine has a rule that salads must contain seven ingredients: greens, protein, cheese, fruit, vegetable, nuts, dressing. She makes delicious salads, but hard-and-fast rules aren't always helpful in a crunch. Cooks pressed for time want to create a delicious mix with ingredients already in the pantry and refrigerator. So the following chart is a general guideline for coming up with your own salad fix. You certainly don't need to incorporate ALL of the following ingredients to make a great mix, but if your refrigerator presents you some leftover chicken, some red leaf lettuce, apples, aged Gouda and pecans, well then, here's guide to building a meal out of those five delicious components.

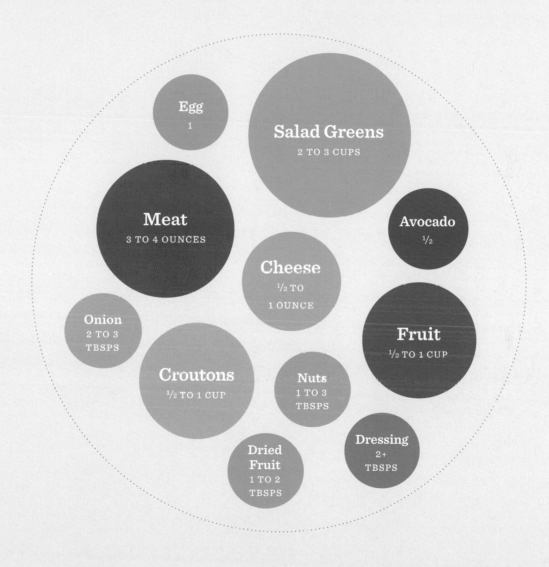

Egg
1

Salad Greens
2 TO 3 CUPS

Meat
3 TO 4 OUNCES

Avocado
1/2

Cheese
1/2 TO
1 OUNCE

Fruit
1/2 TO 1 CUP

Onion
2 TO 3
TBSPS

Croutons
1/2 TO 1 CUP

Nuts
1 TO 3
TBSPS

Dried
Fruit
1 TO 2
TBSPS

Dressing
2+
TBSPS

VEGETARIAN SALADS

Winter Greens and Wild Rice Salad with
Grilled Yams and Lime-Ancho Vinaigrette

Lime-Ancho Vinaigrette

Roasted Acorn Squash and Brussels Sprout
Salad with Quinoa, Pepitas, and Pomegranates

Kale Salad with Wheat Berries, Parmesan,
Pine Nuts, and Currants

Moroccan-Spiced Roasted Cauliflower and
Carrot Salad with Chickpeas and Couscous

Moroccan-Spiced Dressing

Toasted Barley, Long Bean, and Shiitake
Mushroom Salad with Teriyaki Tofu

Baked Teriyaki Tofu Cubes

Tostada Salad with Black Beans, Jicama, and
Queso Fresco with Creamy Lime-Avocado
Dressing and Chile Pepitas

Creamy Lime-Avocado Dressing

Warm Wild Mushroom Salad with
Goat Cheese Toasts

Goat Cheese Toasts

Greek Salad

Oregano Vinaigrette

Poached Eggs with Asparagus and Arugula
with Lemon Vinaigrette, Spring Herbs,
and Parmesan Crostini

Roasted Beet and Blood Orange Salad with
Goat Cheese and Marcona Almonds

Blood Orange–Sherry Vinaigrette

Roasted Beets

Olive Bread Panzanella with Tomatoes,
Kidney Beans, and Lemon

Brown Rice Grape Leaf Salad

Buckwheat Soba Noodles with Sesame Dressing,
Tofu, and Asian Greens

Sesame Dressing

Kohlrabi and Black Quinoa Salad with
Coconut and Cashews

Pea and Orecchiette Salad with
Perlini Mozzarella and Mint

Green Goddess Salad

Green Goddess Dressing

Burrata, Arugula, and Radicchio Pizzette
with Black Olive Vinaigrette

Flatbread Dough

Wilted Swiss Chard Salad with Caramelized
Onions, Croutons, and Fried Eggs

Grilled Eggplant Salad with Heirloom Tomatoes,
Fresh Mozzarella, and Pesto Vinaigrette

Pesto Vinaigrette

Pesto

Chopped Salad with Flatbreads and Labneh

Frisée Salad with Goat Cheese and
Roasted Grapes

Roasted Tomato Salad with Arugula and
Fromage Chacun à Son Goût

Freekeh Salad with Apricots,
Grilled Halloumi, and Zucchini

MY VEGETARIAN SUMMER

I remember the summer my brothers returned from college at Berkeley as vegetarians. As a little kid, I was concerned. Judging from my dad's reaction, they may as well have come home as *commies.* But my mom was game. Maybe she saw it as a fun challenge, a break from the routine of nightly "meat and three." Or perhaps she knew that buying less meat would free up household budget money for trips to the boutique or redecorating. (We did get wild, shiny wallpaper in the breakfast room that year.) She may have taken in my pop's substantial frame and figured that a little less meat would do him good.

Dinner that summer was fun. It was the last year everyone returned home for vacation, and I have fond memories of a lively kitchen full of cooks and big family dinners on the patio. My mom experimented and prepared stuffed zucchini and a cheese grits casserole studded with fresh chilis. She updated her killer enchiladas and burrito recipes to exclude chicken. She even made taco salad without ground beef! My brothers made eggs Florentine, brown rice and mushroom casserole, and pasta salads.

At the end of the summer, my brothers returned to their little house in Oakland. But our family didn't go back to their old ways. The focus shifted away from meat and towards more vegetables, whole grains, legumes, and eggs. Dinner was often centered around a salad. For me the foundation of creating great dinners is simple: showcase fresh ingredients and don't be afraid of vegetarian cooking—a harkening back to my vegetarian summer.

WINTER GREENS AND WILD RICE SALAD
with Grilled Yams and Lime-Ancho Vinaigrette

The nutty flavor of the wild rice and the sweet-smoky quality of the grilled yams combine beautifully in this vegan salad.

1¾ pounds (about 4 thin) dark-fleshed yams, well scrubbed

¾ cup wild rice

½ teaspoon kosher salt

2 celery ribs, sliced

4 green onions, thinly sliced

¼ cup chopped fresh cilantro, plus more for sprinkling

Lime-Ancho Vinaigrette (opposite)

Extra virgin olive oil

12 cups mixed peppery greens, such as arugula, mizuna, red mustard, and spinach

COOK THE YAMS in a large pot of rapidly boiling salted water until almost tender when pierced with a thin sharp knife, about 15 minutes. Drain and let the yams cool completely. *(Yams can be prepared 2 days ahead; cover and refrigerate.)*

Bring the rice, 3 cups water, and salt to a boil in a heavy medium saucepan. Reduce the heat to low, and cover and simmer until the rice is tender and the liquid is absorbed, about 50 minutes. Transfer the rice to a medium bowl and let cool completely.

Add the celery, green onions, ¼ cup cilantro and 3 tablespoons of the vinaigrette to the wild rice and stir well.

Prepare a grill to medium-high heat or preheat a stovetop grill pan over medium-high heat. Cut each cooled yam into quarters lengthwise. Brush the yams with olive oil and season to taste with salt and pepper. Grill the yams until browned and tender, turning occasionally, about 10 minutes.

In a large bowl, toss the greens with 3 tablespoons of the Lime-Ancho Vinaigrette. Divide the greens evenly among 4 plates. Spoon the wild rice salad onto the center of each pile of greens, dividing evenly. Arrange the yams over the rice, dividing evenly. Spoon the remaining dressing over the yams. Sprinkle the salads with the remaining cilantro and serve.

Lime-Ancho Vinaigrette

Ancho chiles are dried poblano chiles. They have a rich, sweet, and mildly piquant flavor. Look for the powder in the spice section of your local grocery store or at Latin American markets. Try the vinaigrette brushed over grilled or steamed corn on the cob in the summertime.

¹/₄ cup freshly squeezed lime juice

1 tablespoon honey

1 generous teaspoon ancho chile powder

1 generous teaspoon ground cumin

1 large garlic clove, pressed

¹/₂ teaspoon kosher salt

¹/₃ cup extra virgin olive oil

WHISK THE LIME juice, honey, chili powder, cumin, garlic, and salt in a small bowl to blend. Gradually whisk in the olive oil. *(Can be prepared 3 days ahead. Cover and refrigerate.)*

ROASTED ACORN SQUASH AND BRUSSELS SPROUT SALAD
with Quinoa, Pepitas, and Pomegranates

4 SERVINGS

This salad blends my fall-produce favorites with protein-packed quinoa. Quinoa is an ancient grain that is native to South America. It comes in golden, red, and black varieties, with the golden variety being the most readily available and delicately flavored. You can purchase quinoa, along with the pepitas (hulled, toasted pumpkin seeds) at a natural foods store. Pomegranate molasses adds a robust sweet-tart flavor to the vinaigrette—find it at Middle Eastern markets or from an online purveyor. It's not necessary to peel the acorn squash, as the skin is edible.

VINAIGRETTE

1/4 cup minced shallot

3 tablespoons extra virgin olive oil

1 1/2 tablespoons apple cider vinegar

1 1/2 tablespoons pomegranate molasses

2 garlic cloves, pressed

1/2 teaspoon kosher salt

SALAD

2 cups vegetable broth

1 cup quinoa

1 pound Brussels sprouts, cut in half

3 tablespoons extra virgin olive oil, divided

1 (1- to 1 1/4-pound) acorn squash, cut into 16 wedges

1 teaspoon ground coriander

1/2 teaspoon ground allspice

1/2 teaspoon paprika

1/2 teaspoon kosher salt

1/4 cup chopped fresh Italian parsley

1/2 cup pepitas, toasted

1 cup (about) pomegranate seeds, from 1 pomegranate or 1 (5.3-ounce) package

FOR THE VINAIGRETTE: Whisk the shallot, oil, vinegar, pomegranate molasses, garlic, and salt to blend in a small bowl.

For the salad: Bring the broth and the quinoa to a boil over medium-high heat; reduce the heat and simmer until the liquid is reduced by half, about 10 minutes. Reduce the heat to low, and cover and cook until the quinoa is tender and the liquid is absorbed, about 10 minutes. Remove the quinoa from the heat and set aside.

Position one rack in the lower third and one rack in the upper third of the oven and preheat to 450°F. Brush 2 heavy large baking sheets with olive oil. Toss the Brussels sprouts with 2 tablespoons olive oil in a medium bowl. Arrange the Brussels sprouts, cut side down, on one prepared baking sheet. Toss the squash with the remaining 1 tablespoon olive oil, coriander, allspice, paprika, and salt in the same medium bowl. Arrange the squash in a single layer on the second prepared baking sheet. Roast the Brussels sprouts on the bottom the squash in a single layer on the second prepared baking sheet. Roast the Brussels sprouts on the bottom rack and the squash on the top rack of the oven until the Brussels sprouts are well browned on the bottom and tender when pierced with a sharp knife and the squash is tender, about 15 minutes.

Stir the Italian parsley, toasted pepitas, and 2 tablespoons of the vinaigrette into the quinoa. Divide the quinoa among 4 plates.

Return the Brussels sprouts to the same medium bowl and toss with 1 tablespoon vinaigrette. Spoon the Brussels sprouts over the quinoa, dividing evenly. Divide the squash wedges among the plates. Sprinkle the salads with the pomegranate seeds, drizzle with the remaining dressing, and serve.

KALE SALAD
with Wheat Berries, Parmesan, Pine Nuts, and Currants

I don't know for certain if Dan Barber of NYC's Blue Hill restaurant invented the kale salad, but I'll give him credit anyway. I came across his version when I was testing recipes for *Bon Appétit* magazine. While many chefs' recipes are notorious for not working—it can be a challenge to translate restaurant proportions to something that makes sense for home cooking—this was not the case with Chef Barber's recipes. Each and every one not only worked perfectly as written, but was a revelation—especially when it came to preparing vegetables. While cooking, I felt like I was participating in some sort of culinary master class. A while later, I made a pilgrimage to his Greenwich Village restaurant and to the educational farm at Stone Barns in Pocanto Hills. So this is my homage to Dan Barber's kale salad, amped up with a few wheat berries to make it suitable for serving as a main dish.

2/3 cup farro or semi-pearled wheat berries

1/3 cup extra virgin olive oil

3 to 4 tablespoons freshly squeezed lemon juice

2 tablespoons white balsamic vinegar

1 tablespoon honey

1/2 teaspoon kosher salt

2 bunches (each about 12 ounces) kale, ribs removed, leaves roughly chopped into 1-inch pieces (about 12 to 14 cups)

1/4 cup grated Parmesan cheese

3 tablespoons toasted pine nuts

2 tablespoons currants

COOK THE FARRO in a medium pot of rapidly boiling salted water until just tender, about 30 minutes. Drain the farro and let cool completely. (*The farro can be cooked up to 1 day ahead; cover and refrigerate.*)

In a large bowl, combine the olive oil, 3 tablespoons lemon juice, vinegar, honey, and salt and whisk to blend. Add the kale and stir to coat well. Let the salad stand 1 hour or overnight.

Mix the salad well, adding additional lemon juice to taste. Stir in the farro, cheese, pine nuts and currants. Season the salad with freshly ground black pepper and serve.

TOASTED BARLEY, LONG BEAN, AND SHIITAKE MUSHROOM SALAD with Teriyaki Tofu

Nutty barley, earthy mushrooms, teriyaki tofu, and long beans combine in a Japanese-inspired salad. Long beans, sometimes called asparagus beans, resemble regular green beans, but they grow to be more than a foot long and have a more pliable texture. Look for them at some supermarkets or at Asian markets. If you are short on time, substitute a 7- or 8-ounce package of teriyaki-flavored baked tofu.

DRESSING

¼ cup unseasoned rice wine vinegar

2 tablespoons toasted sesame oil

2 tablespoons soy sauce

1 tablespoon brown sugar

2 teaspoons finely grated peeled fresh ginger

1 garlic clove, pressed

SALAD

2 tablespoons toasted sesame oil, divided, plus more for brushing

1 cup pearled barley

½ teaspoon kosher salt

1 pound long beans (1 bunch) or green beans, trimmed and cut into 1-inch pieces

10 ounces large shiitake mushrooms, stems trimmed to the cap and discarded

Baked Teriyaki Tofu Cubes (opposite)

6 green onions, trimmed and thinly sliced

FOR THE DRESSING: Whisk the vinegar, sesame oil, soy sauce, brown sugar, ginger, and garlic to blend in a small bowl. Set aside.

For the salad: Heat 1 tablespoon sesame oil in a heavy medium saucepan over medium-high heat. Add the barley and stir until lightly toasted, about 3 minutes. Add 5 cups water and ½ teaspoon kosher salt and bring to a boil. Reduce the heat to medium-low and simmer until the barley is tender, about 45 minutes. Drain and cool completely.

Heat the remaining 1 tablespoon sesame oil in a heavy large skillet. Add the long beans and ¼ cup water. Sprinkle lightly with salt and cook until the beans are crisp-tender and the water has evaporated, about 3 minutes. Cool the beans to room temperature.

Prepare a grill to medium-high heat or preheat a stovetop grill pan over medium-high heat. Brush the mushrooms with sesame oil and place on the grill, oiled side down. Season the mushrooms lightly with salt and cook until browned on bottom, about 7 minutes. Turn and continue cooking until tender when pierced with a small sharp knife, about 7 minutes longer. Cool and thinly slice each crosswise.

In a large bowl, combine the barley, beans, mushrooms, tofu, and green onions. Add the dressing and stir to combine. *(Can be prepared 1 day ahead. Cover and refrigerate.)*

Baked Teriyaki Tofu Cubes

Removing excess moisture from the tofu by pressing gently between towels makes the cubes firm enough for baking without falling apart. Enjoy these sweet-salty cubes as a snack.

1 (12-ounce) package extra-firm tofu, drained

2 tablespoons (packed) golden brown sugar

2 tablespoons soy sauce

1 teaspoon finely grated peeled fresh ginger

1 garlic clove, pressed

1 teaspoon toasted sesame oil

LINE A LARGE rimmed baking sheet with a clean dish towel. Cut the block of tofu into five 1-inch-thick slices. Arrange slices on towel and fold in edges of towel to enclose tofu. Top with another baking sheet. Place a few cans of food atop the second sheet for weight and let stand 30 minutes.

Cut each tofu slice into 10 cubes (about $1/2$- to $3/4$ inch cubes). Combine the brown sugar, soy sauce, ginger, and garlic in small, shallow baking dish. Add the cubes and stir gently to coat. Let stand until marinade is completely absorbed, about 10 minutes.

Preheat the oven to 375°F. Brush a heavy large baking sheet with the sesame oil. Arrange the tofu cubes in a single layer on the prepared baking sheet. Bake until the tofu is browned on all sides, stirring 3 times, about 30 minutes. Let the tofu cubes cool before using.

TOSTADA SALAD

with Black Beans, Jicama, and Queso Fresco with Creamy Lime-Avocado Dressing and Chile Pepitas

6 SERVINGS

This is a big, messy salad with crisp tortilla chips, crunchy-sweet jicama, creamy avocados, and a luscious lime-kissed dressing. If you are pressed for time, you can use 3 cups purchased tortilla chips instead of the freshly fried. Queso fresco is crumbly cow's milk cheese with a mild flavor that's available at most supermarkets. French feta can be substituted for the queso.

2 teaspoons corn oil plus additional for frying

1/2 cup pepitas

1/2 teaspoon ancho chile powder or regular chili powder

1/4 teaspoon kosher salt

6 corn tortillas

12 cups romaine hearts, cut crosswise into 1-inch pieces

12 ounces (about 1 half) jicama, peeled and cut into 1/2x2-inch pieces

1 bunch radishes, trimmed and sliced

1/2 pint cherry tomatoes, cut in half

1 (15-ounce) can black beans, rinsed and drained

1/2 red onion, very thinly sliced

Creamy Lime-Avocado Dressing (opposite)

8 ounces crumbled queso fresco

1/3 cup chopped fresh cilantro

HEAT 2 TEASPOONS corn oil in a heavy small skillet over medium-high heat. Add the pepitas, chile powder, and 1/4 teaspoon kosher salt and stir until the pepitas are golden brown and beginning to pop, about 2 minutes. Remove from the heat and let cool completely. *(The chile pepitas can be made 3 days ahead. Store in a jar at room temperature.)*

Stack the tortillas and cut in half. Cut the halved tortillas crosswise into 3/4-inch strips. Fill a heavy deep skillet with 1 inch of corn oil and heat over medium-high heat until very hot. Reduce heat to medium and, working in batches, add tortilla pieces to the oil and fry, turning once, until the tortillas are golden and crisp, about 1 minute per batch. Transfer the tortillas to a brown paper bag or paper towels to drain. Sprinkle the tortilla strips with salt to taste. *(The tortillas strips can be made 8 hours ahead. Cover loosely and store at room temperature.)*

In a large bowl, combine the lettuce, jicama, radishes, tomatoes, black beans, and red onion in a large bowl. Add the tortilla chips and enough Creamy Lime-Avocado Dressing to season to taste and toss to combine. Sprinkle the salad with the cheese, chile pepitas, and cilantro and serve.

Creamy Lime-Avocado Dressing

This thick and creamy dressing makes a great dip for crudités, corn chips, or cooked shrimp.

½ avocado, pitted

½ cup chopped fresh cilantro

½ cup pepitas, toasted

6 tablespoons extra virgin olive oil

6 tablespoons freshly squeezed lime juice plus additional if necessary

1 jalapeño pepper, stemmed and seeded

1 garlic clove, peeled

½ teaspoon kosher salt

COMBINE ALL THE ingredients in a blender and purée until smooth. *(Dressing can be prepared 1 day ahead. Cover and refrigerate. Thin the dressing with additional lime juice and olive oil if necessary.)*

WARM WILD MUSHROOM SALAD
with Goat Cheese Toasts

On a recent trip to the farmers' market, I found ruffled school-bus-yellow chanterelles displayed in large, unceremonious piles. At $9.99 a pound, I had to get a big paper bagful. Nine-ninety-nine a pound? That might sound pricey, but it's a bargain. A pound of mushrooms is plenty, and richly flavored, meaty wild mushrooms are worthy of a special meal—especially when enriched with a splash of cream and accompanied by goat cheese toasts. I fashioned this salad with chanterelle mushrooms, but any mix of wild mushrooms will do. Using a fresh, local goat cheese sold at your farmers' market along with local greens makes this a showcase locavore recipe—and another great reason to get out to your neighborhood farmstand or farmers' markets.

3½ tablespoons extra virgin olive oil, divided

1 pound wild mushrooms, such as chanterelles, thickly sliced (about 8 cups)

2 tablespoons minced shallot

4 garlic cloves, minced

1 teaspoon chopped fresh thyme leaves

¼ cup dry white wine

¼ cup plus 1½ tablespoons whipping cream, divided

1 tablespoon white wine vinegar

¼ teaspoon kosher salt

12 cups mixed baby greens

Goat Cheese Toasts (opposite)

HEAT 2 TABLESPOONS olive oil in a heavy large well-seasoned cast-iron or nonstick skillet over medium-high heat. Add the mushrooms and sauté until they are moist in appearance and begin to become tender, about 8 minutes. Add the shallots, garlic, and thyme and continue to sauté until the shallots and garlic are tender, about 4 minutes. Pour the wine over the mushrooms and sauté until the wine evaporates, about 3 minutes. Add ¼ cup cream to the mushrooms and sprinkle them with a little kosher salt and sauté until the mushrooms and tender and lightly coated, about 4 minutes. Season the mushrooms to taste with salt and pepper.

Meanwhile, whisk the remaining 1½ tablespoons olive oil and 1½ tablespoons cream to blend in a large bowl. Whisk in the white wine vinegar and ¼ teaspoon kosher salt. Add the salad greens to the large bowl and toss until coated. Divide the salad greens among 4 plates. Top the greens with the warm mushrooms, dividing evenly. Surround the mushrooms with Goat Cheese Toasts and serve.

Goat Cheese Toasts

These warm, crunchy toasts can be served on their own as an appetizer—they're especially good with a small spoonful of black-cherry preserves and an additional sprinkling of fresh thyme leaves.

16 slices from French bread baguette

Extra virgin olive oil

6 to 8 ounces soft fresh goat cheese, room temperature

1 teaspoon chopped fresh thyme leaves

PREHEAT THE OVEN to 400°F. Arrange baguette slices on a heavy large rimmed baking sheet. Brush the slices lightly with olive oil and bake in the oven until lightly toasted, about 7 minutes. Let toasts cool. *(Toasted baguette slices can be made 2 days ahead. Store them in a resealable plastic bag at room temperature.)*

Preheat the oven to 400°F. Spread the toasts thickly with goat cheese and arrange on a heavy large rimmed baking sheet. Sprinkle the toasts with thyme and freshly ground black pepper. Bake until the goat cheese is hot, about 7 minutes.

UMAMI

Sweet, sour, bitter, salty. Salads feature those four taste sensations in one big bowl. Yet salad also serves as a showcase for the fifth taste—umami, or savoriness. Cured meats (bacon!), fish, shellfish, aged cheeses, mushrooms, tomatoes, cabbage, soy sauce, fish sauce, and spinach all tantalize the taste buds in the same way. They are umami, and they coat the tongue with pleasant meaty, brothlike fullness. When umami is combined with the other tastes, especially salty, it creates a super-blend, or knockout mix. That could be why so many of us crave a good salad.

GREEK SALAD

This slightly amped-up version of the classic Greek village salad is one of my favorites. It's hard to go wrong with the combo of fresh greens, ripe tomatoes, salty olives and feta, and cool, crisp cucumber.

16 to 20 leaves of romaine lettuce, trimmed

4 Persian cucumbers, sliced, or
2 cucumbers, peeled and sliced

4 small tomatoes, cut into wedges

1 red bell pepper, sliced

½ red onion, thinly sliced

8 ounces feta cheese, crumbled

¾ cup pitted kalamata olives, halved
lengthwise

1 tablespoon drained capers, chopped

Oregano Vinaigrette (below)

¼ cup fresh Italian parsley leaves (optional)

LINE 4 PLATES with the lettuce leaves. Top the lettuce on each plate with cucumbers, tomatoes, red bell pepper, red onion, feta, and olives, dividing evenly. Add the capers to the Oregano Vinaigrette and whisk to blend. Spoon the dressing over salads. Season the salads with freshly ground black pepper, sprinkle with the parsley leaves, if using, and serve.

Oregano Vinaigrette

You can make this multipurpose vinaigrette with fresh or dried oregano.

3 tablespoons red wine vinegar

1 garlic clove, pressed

1 tablespoon chopped fresh oregano or
1 teaspoon dried, crumbled

¼ teaspoon kosher salt

⅛ teaspoon crushed red pepper

½ cup extra virgin olive oil

WHISK THE VINEGAR, garlic, oregano, salt, and crushed red pepper to blend in a small bowl. Gradually whisk in the oil.

POACHED EGGS with Asparagus and Arugula with Lemon Vinaigrette, Spring Herbs, and Parmesan Crostini

This is a perky salad that's perfect for a springtime brunch. Use a blend of the suggested herbs below or any mix of spring herbs that have sprung up in your garden or window box. To save on dishes and time, just poach the eggs in the same simmering water used to cook the asparagus.

1½ pounds asparagus, trimmed

1 tablespoon white wine vinegar

4 eggs

12 cups arugula

Lemon Vinaigrette (page 85)

3 tablespoons chopped fresh "spring" herbs, such as cilantro, chives, dill, mint, and tarragon

Parmesan Crostini (page 108)

FILL A LARGE skillet with 1 inch of salted water and bring to a simmer over high heat. Add the asparagus, and cover and cook until crisp-tender, about 2 minutes. Using tongs, transfer the asparagus to a bowl of ice water to cool. Drain the asparagus and pat dry with a clean dish towel.

Return the skillet of water to a gentle simmer. Add the vinegar to the water. Working one at a time, crack an egg into a small bowl and gently slide the egg into the simmering water in the skillet. Poach the eggs, gently pushing simmering water over the tops, until the whites are cooked through but the yolks are not set, about 3 minutes. Carefully remove the eggs from the water with a slotted spoon and drain.

Working quickly, toss the arugula with 4 tablespoons of the Lemon Vinaigrette and 2 tablespoons chopped fresh herbs in a large bowl. Divide the dressed greens among 4 plates. Top the arugula with the asparagus, dividing evenly. Carefully place the eggs atop the asparagus. Sprinkle the remaining tablespoon of chopped herbs over the eggs and the asparagus. Season the eggs with freshly ground black pepper and sea salt. Drizzle the salads with the remaining vinaigrette and serve with Parmesan Crostini.

ROASTED BEET AND BLOOD ORANGE SALAD
with Goat Cheese and Marcona Almonds

⎯| 2 SERVINGS

Roasted beets and sweet citrus taste great when combined with creamy goat cheese and crunchy almonds. Marcona almonds are a tender almond variety with delicate sweetness and a squat, teardrop shape. They are traditionally sold blanched and fried in olive oil. I like to make this salad with the ruby-colored blood oranges that grow in my backyard, but it's also wonderful with sweet tangerines or small navel oranges. Serve the salad with whole grain baguette. If you are able to get your hands on puntarelle lettuce, this salad would be an excellent way to showcase it.

6 cups mixed red greens and/or arugula

4 roasted beets (page 56), peeled and sliced

4 small blood oranges, peeled, pith removed, and sliced, or tangerines, peeled and separated into sections

3 ounces soft, fresh goat cheese, crumbled

¼ cup Marcona almonds

Blood Orange-Sherry Vinaigrette (below)

ARRANGE THE SALAD greens attractively on 2 dinner plates, dividing evenly. Top the greens with the beet and orange slices. Scatter the goat cheese over the salads, dividing evenly. Sprinkle the salads with the almonds and serve, allowing both diners to spoon the Blood Orange-Sherry Vinaigrette over their own salads.

Blood Orange–Sherry Vinaigrette

⎯| MAKES ABOUT ½ CUP

If making a salad with tangerines or navel oranges, substitute tangerine or navel orange peel and juice for the blood orange. Enjoy this dressing over mixed sliced citrus adorned with parsley leaves.

3 tablespoons finely chopped shallot

1 tablespoon freshly squeezed blood orange juice

1 tablespoon sherry vinegar

¼ teaspoon kosher salt

¼ teaspoon grated blood orange peel

¼ teaspoon sugar

3 tablespoons extra virgin olive oil

IN A SMALL bowl, stir the shallot, orange juice, vinegar, salt, orange peel, and sugar to blend. Whisk in the olive oil to blend.

Roasted Beets

Roasted beets are a sweet and earthy addition to salads. If you like beets, consider doubling the recipe, as the cooked beets will keep in the refrigerator for about a week . To store the beets, simply cool and transfer them whole and unpeeled to a resealable plastic bag. The skin slips off the beets easily when you're ready to use them. If you want to avoid pink-stained hands, wear latex gloves or lightly coat your fingertips with vegetable oil.

1 bunch of beets (about 3 to 4 beets), trimmed

Vegetable oil

PREHEAT THE OVEN to 375°F.

Arrange the beets in roasting pan that is just large enough to accommodate them. Drizzle the beets with small amount of vegetable oil and turn to coat beets in oil. Cover the pan with foil. Roast the beets in the oven until tender when pierced with a thin, sharp knife, about 1 hour. Cool. *(Beets can be roasted 6 days ahead; refrigerate.)*

OLIVE BREAD PANZANELLA
with Tomatoes, Kidney Beans, and Lemon

Panzanella is an Italian dish that makes use of stale bread and extra-ripe tomatoes. The herb-and-garlic-infused tomato juices soak into the bread, moistening and flavoring it. Here, the salad takes an eastern Mediterranean turn with lots of lemon and feta, which transforms it into a filling summer supper.

10 ounces olive bread, cut into ½-inch cubes (about 6 cups)

2 pounds best-quality ripe tomatoes, cored and cut into wedges

8 tablespoons extra virgin olive oil, divided

4 to 6 tablespoons freshly squeezed lemon juice

3 garlic cloves, pressed

½ teaspoon kosher salt

1 (14-ounce) can red kidney beans, rinsed and drained

3 Persian cucumbers, cut into rounds

3 green onions, thinly sliced

2 tablespoons chopped fresh oregano

2 tablespoons chopped fresh cilantro

2 teaspoons cumin seed

5 cups mixed greens, such as spinach, romaine, and arugula, torn into pieces

3 ounces feta cheese, crumbled

PREHEAT THE OVEN to 400°F. Spread the bread cubes in a single layer on a very large rimmed baking sheet. Bake in the oven until lightly toasted, stirring once or twice, about 15 minutes. Let cool. (Bread cubes can be prepared up to 2 days ahead. Cool completely and store in an airtight jar or bag.)

In a large bowl, combine the tomatoes, 6 tablespoons olive oil, 4 tablespoons lemon juice, and garlic. Sprinkle with ½ teaspoon kosher salt and let stand until very juicy, about 30 minutes

Add the red kidney beans, bread, cucumbers, green onions, oregano, and cilantro to the tomatoes and let the salad stand until the bread softens slightly, about 10 minutes.

Meanwhile, stir the cumin seed in a small skillet over medium-high heat until fragrant and lightly toasted, about 1 minute. Cool completely.

Add the greens to the salad and toss gently to combine. Season to taste with salt and with the remaining 1 to 2 tablespoons lemon juice if desired. Sprinkle the salad with feta and toasted cumin seed and serve.

BROWN RICE GRAPE LEAF SALAD

The best flavors and textures of a good dolma—a Mediterranean stuffed grape leaf mezze—combine in a salad that is more fun to make and eat than the individually stuffed appetizer. Grape leaves packed in brine are available at Middle Eastern markets or online. In a pinch, you could substitute a couple of tablespoons of rinsed and finely chopped capers to mimic the mild pickle-y taste of the grape leaves. I serve the rice salad on a bed of greens, but it's also a great side on its own.

1 cup brown rice, rinsed, or 10.5-ounce package fully cooked brown rice

1/2 teaspoon kosher salt (if needed)

3 tablespoons extra virgin olive oil, divided

2 tablespoons fresh lemon juice, divided

1/2 cup currants

1/2 cup dry-roasted shelled pistachios or toasted pine nuts

1/3 cup finely chopped, rinsed, and drained brined grape leaves (about 12)

1/4 cup thinly sliced green onions

1/2 cup crumbled feta cheese (about 1 1/2 ounces)

2 tablespoons minced fresh cilantro

2 tablespoons minced fresh dill

2 tablespoons minced fresh mint

6 cups arugula or mixed greens

1 1/3 cups (about) plain Greek yogurt

Lemon wedges

IF USING UNCOOKED rice: Bring 2 cups water to a boil in a heavy medium saucepan. Add the rice and 1/2 teaspoon kosher salt. Return the water to a boil and reduce heat to very low. Cover and simmer until the rice is tender and the water is absorbed, about 40 minutes. Remove from the heat and let stand, covered, 5 minutes. Transfer the rice to a bowl and stir in 1 tablespoon olive oil and 1 tablespoon lemon juice and let cool to room temperature.

If using packaged rice: Place the rice in a large microwave-safe bowl. Add 1 tablespoon water. Cover and microwave on high 1 minute or until rice softens. Mix in 1 tablespoon olive oil and 1 tablespoon lemon juice.

Stir the currants, nuts, chopped grape leaves, green onions, feta, cilantro, dill, and mint into the cooled rice.

In a separate large bowl, toss the arugula with the remaining 2 tablespoons olive oil and 1 tablespoon lemon juice. Season the greens to taste with salt. Divide the greens among 4 plates and top with the rice salad, dividing evenly. Spoon a dollop of yogurt alongside the salad; garnish with lemon wedges, and serve.

BUCKWHEAT SOBA NOODLES
with Sesame Dressing, Tofu, and Asian Greens

On a hot day, an iced tea or beer is the perfect thing to drink with these cold, silky buckwheat noodles, especially when they are coated with a toasty, gingery sesame dressing. Buckwheat soba noodles have a unique nutty flavor. If you can't find them, you can try substituting another variety of soba or use spaghetti.

8 to 9 ounces buckwheat soba noodles

Sesame Dressing (below)

4 cups mixed Asian greens, such as mizuna and tatsoi

1 Japanese cucumber or 2 Persian cucumbers, cut in half and thinly sliced on a diagonal

4 green onions, thinly sliced

4 (1-inch-thick) slices soft tofu (about 8 ounces), cut into ½-inch cubes

Toasted sesame seeds

BRING A LARGE shallow pot of water to boil over high heat. Add the noodles and boil until tender but still firm to the bite, about 5 minutes. Drain the noodles. Rinse the noodles with cold water to cool and drain well. Transfer the noodles to a medium bowl and stir in ⅓ cup Sesame Dressing.

In a large bowl, toss the greens, cucumber, and green onions with enough Sesame Dressing to coat and season to taste.

Divide the greens evenly among 4 bowls. Spoon the noodles over the greens, dividing evenly. Top the noodles with tofu cubes. Drizzle a small amount of dressing over the tofu. Sprinkle the salads with sesame seeds and serve.

Sesame Dressing

Try this over sliced cucumbers with a sprinkle of sesame seeds for a light snack or appetizer.

⅓ cup toasted sesame oil

⅓ cup rice wine vinegar

2 tablespoons brown sugar

2 tablespoons soy sauce

2 tablespoons tahini (sesame seed paste)

4 teaspoons grated peeled fresh ginger

2 garlic cloves, pressed

WHISK ALL THE ingredients to blend in a medium bowl. *(Dressing can be prepared up to 3 days ahead and refrigerated.)*

KOHLRABI AND BLACK QUINOA SALAD
with Coconut and Cashews

Kohlrabi is a member of the cabbage family. The baseball-sized vegetable with a few leafy top pieces can be eaten cooked or raw. I like kohlrabi best raw—its flavor and texture remind me of sweeter, crunchier broccoli stems. Combining kohlrabi with coconut milk and ginger brings out the sweetness of the vegetable in this refreshing vegan salad. Cooking the super nutritious, nutty-flavored black quinoa in coconut milk infuses it with extra sweetness. The black grains lend an exotic look to the salad, but you can use red or gold quinoa if desired. Look for black quinoa and the unsweetened coconut flakes at a natural foods market.

1 (14-ounce) can light coconut milk, divided

½ teaspoon kosher salt

1 cup black quinoa

3 (about 1 bunch) kohlrabi, tops trimmed, bulbs peeled and cut into matchstick-sized strips

2 green onions, thinly sliced

¼ cup finely chopped fresh cilantro

1 jalapeño pepper, stemmed, seeded, and minced

2 tablespoons freshly squeezed lime juice

2 teaspoons grated peeled fresh ginger

½ cup roasted cashew pieces

¼ cup dried unsweetened grated coconut

MEASURE 1½ CUPS of the coconut milk (reserve the remainder for the dressing) into a heavy medium saucepan. Add 1 cup water and the salt to the coconut milk and bring to a simmer over medium heat. Add the quinoa, reduce the heat to medium-low, and simmer until the liquid is reduced by half, about 15 minutes. Cover and simmer until all the liquid is absorbed and the quinoa is tender, about 10 minutes longer. Transfer the quinoa to a large bowl and let stand until cooled to room temperature.

Add the kohlrabi, green onions, cilantro, and jalapeno to the quinoa and toss to combine. In a small bowl, stir the remaining coconut milk, lime juice, and ginger to blend for the dressing. Pour the dressing over the salad and toss to combine. Stir the cashews and coconut into the salad and serve.

PEA AND ORECCHIETTE SALAD
with Perlini Mozzarella and Mint

4 SERVINGS

English peas and snap peas are featured in this springtime pasta salad. Perlini are little pea-sized balls of fresh mozzarella. The peas and the perlini fall neatly into the pockets of the "little ear" (orecchiette) or shell pasta. I like to use mild green garlic in this salad as it appears in the garden and at the farmers' markets at the same time as the peas do, but you can use a clove of garlic instead. Pea tendrils, the tender leafy tops of pea plants, are sold at farmers' markets in spring or can be found at Chinese markets (they're a popular addition to stir-fries). I like to remove the tender, pea-flavored leaves from the tendrils and enjoy them as an addition to salads.

10 ounces fresh, shucked English peas (about 2 cups), or 2 cups thawed frozen peas

6 ounces sugar snap peas or snow pea pods (about 2 cups)

6 ounces orecchiette or conchiglie (shell) pasta (about 2 cups)

4 tablespoons extra virgin olive oil, divided

3 tablespoons white balsamic vinegar, divided

1 tablespoon minced green garlic or 1 garlic clove, pressed

1 (8-ounce) container perlini (fresh mozzarella pearls), drained

1 cup pea leaves or baby spinach leaves

2 green onions, thinly sliced

2 tablespoons minced fresh mint

BRING A LARGE saucepan of generously salted water to a boil. Add both peas and boil until just tender, about 1½ minutes. Using a slotted spoon, transfer the peas to a colander set over a bowl (maintain boiling water in the saucepan). Rinse the peas briefly under cold water to cool. Drain well.

Add the pasta to the boiling water and cook until tender but still firm to the bite, about 10 minutes. Drain the pasta (do not rinse) and transfer it to a large bowl.

Add 2 tablespoons of olive oil, 1 tablespoon of vinegar, and the garlic to the hot pasta and stir to combine. Let the pasta stand until it cools to room temperature.

Add the peas, perlini, pea leaves, green onions, and mint to the pasta. Add the remaining 2 tablespoons olive oil and 2 tablespoons vinegar. Season the salad to taste with salt and pepper and mix well. Serve at room temperature.

GREEN GODDESS SALAD

I am lucky that the closest restaurant to my home is a wonderful little place that is famous for its sea-salt caramels. Aside from her fabulous sweets, Christine at the Little Flower Candy Company makes delicious sandwiches and salads. The Goddess Salad is one of her most popular. While the Goddess Salad at Little Flower is dressed with a lemon-thyme vinaigrette, I just couldn't resist merging Christine's Goddess with a tangy green goddess dressing and juicy green zebra tomatoes.

8 ounces haricots verts (thin French green beans), trimmed

12 cups mixed greens

2 Persian cucumbers, sliced

2 tomatoes, preferably green zebra or yellow tomatoes, sliced into thin wedges

4 hardboiled eggs (page 97)

4 ounces feta cheese, crumbled

Green Goddess Dressing (page 66)

COOK THE HARICOTS verts in a saucepan of rapidly boiling salted water until they are crisp-tender, about 3 minutes. Transfer them to a bowl of ice water to cool rapidly. Drain the beans well and pat dry with a clean dish towel. *(Haricots verts can be prepared up to 2 days ahead; cover and refrigerate.)*

Divide the greens among 4 large individual salad bowls. Arrange the haricots verts, cucumbers, and tomatoes in sections atop the greens. Using a cheese grater, grate 1 hardboiled egg onto each salad. Sprinkle the salads with the feta cheese and serve with the Green Goddess Dressing.

Green Goddess Dressing

There was a time before my mom started making salad dressings from scratch when I was allowed to choose any kind of bottled dressing I wanted at the supermarket. I always picked green goddess. As I was a little girl, I think the whole goddess thing was a big part of the appeal, but even by the age of six I had acquired quite a taste for chives (chive cottage cheese being the only form of curds that I would eat). I don't buy the bottled version anymore, but a taste of the homemade reminds me why this delicious dressing, created at San Francisco's Palace Hotel in the '20s, has never really gone out of style. Anchovies are in it, but if you plan on serving this to vegetarians, capers make a worthy stand-in.

½ cup sour cream

¼ cup freshly squeezed lemon juice

¼ cup mayonnaise

¼ cup snipped chives

¼ cup chopped fresh tarragon

2 garlic cloves, peeled

2 teaspoons chopped anchovy
(about 2 fillets)

½ teaspoon kosher salt

COMBINE ALL OF the ingredients in a blender and puree until smooth. Season the dressing to taste with salt and pepper. *(The dressing can be prepared 3 days ahead. Cover and refrigerate.)*

PERSIAN CUCUMBERS

You might notice that in many of the recipes calling for cucumber, I specify a Persian cucumber. If you are not familiar with Persian cukes, go and meet one right away. Persian cucumbers are smaller than the standard slicing variety; generally, they are about six inches long and an inch in diameter. These delicate cukes have thin, edible skin and are nearly seedless. Peeling or seeding is not required. The Persian cucumber has the sweetest flavor of any cucumber I have tasted and the coolest crunch. It used to be that I could only find Persian cucumbers at my local farmers' market or at the Middle Eastern produce store. Now my neighborhood supermarket carries them almost year-round.

BURRATA, ARUGULA, AND RADICCHIO
PIZZETTE with Black Olive Vinaigrette

Freshly baked individual pizzas are topped with creamy burrata, black olives, and a colorful salad. Think of burrata as mozzarella's rich relative—a shell of fresh mozzarella is filled with fresh cream and cheese curds. (*Burrata* means "buttered" in Italian.) You can generally find burrata where fresh mozzarella is sold. If it's unavailable, go ahead and use mozzarella on this fun, pizza-like salad. In the recipe, I say to "slice" the burratta, which is a little like slicing a cream-filled balloon. The slices won't be perfect, but it's okay as the whole pie gets topped with the dressed greens.

BLACK OLIVE VINAIGRETTE

2 tablespoons pitted oil-cured black olives

3 tablespoons extra virgin olive oil

1 tablespoon balsamic vinegar

1 garlic clove, minced

$1/2$ teaspoon fresh thyme leaves or pinch of dried thyme

$1/8$ teaspoon crushed red pepper

PIZZETTE

2 tablespoons pitted oil-cured black olives

1 recipe Flatbread Dough (page 69)

2 cups arugula leaves

$3/4$ cup bite-sized pieces radicchio, from about $1/2$ small head

8 ounces burrata (about 1 ball), sliced

FOR THE DRESSING: Finely chop the olives. Transfer the chopped olives to a small bowl and whisk in the oil, vinegar, garlic, thyme, and crushed red pepper. Season the vinaigrette with freshly ground pepper.

For the pizzette: Slice the olives into rounds and set aside. Preheat the oven to 450°F. Divide the flatbread dough into 2 even rounds. Roll out the rounds on a lightly floured surface until they measure approximately 7 inches in diameter. Lightly dust both sides of the rounds with flour. Transfer them to a heavy baking sheet. Bake the rounds until brown spots appear on the bottom and golden brown spots appear on the top, about 10 minutes.

Meanwhile, toss the arugula and the radicchio with half of the vinaigrette.

Remove the pizzette from the oven and immediately top with the burrata slices and sliced black olives, dividing evenly. Drizzle the remaining vinaigrette over the cheese and transfer the pizzette to plates. Top with the salad and serve.

Flatbread Dough

This is enough dough to make two individual pizzas (pizzette) or small flatbreads, or one 12-inch pizza.

$1/2$ teaspoon active dry yeast

1 cup unbleached all-purpose flour

1 tablespoon vital wheat gluten flour

1 teaspoon sugar

$1/2$ teaspoon kosher salt

1 teaspoon extra virgin olive oil

WHISK THE YEAST with $1/3$ cup lukewarm water to blend in a 1-cup measuring cup and let stand 5 minutes. Combine the flour, wheat gluten, sugar, and salt in a food processor; pulse to blend. Whisk the olive oil into the yeast mixture. With the processor running, pour the yeast mixture through the feed tube and process until the dough forms a ball, about 1 minute. (If the dough does not form a ball, add water by teaspoonfuls until the dough comes together to form a ball.)

Turn the dough out onto a lightly floured surface and knead it briefly, about 2 minutes. Lightly brush a large bowl with olive oil. Transfer the dough to the prepared bowl and turn to coat lightly. Cover the bowl tightly with a lid or plastic wrap. Let the dough proof in a warm, draft-free area until doubled in volume, about 1 hour.

(Dough can be prepared 2 days ahead. Transfer the dough to a resealable plastic bag, seal tightly, and refrigerate. Allow the dough to come to room temperature before using, about 1 hour at warm room temperature.)

WILTED SWISS CHARD SALAD
with Caramelized Onions, Croutons, and Fried Eggs

Chard is one of the easiest greens to grow. For that reason, *and* because I love it so much, it's always present in my garden. In fact, there are times when chard is the only veggie producing, so I have come up with multiple ways to enjoy this healthful and prolific plant. Here, I combine it with fresh eggs for a warm and comforting dish that can be made with just one skillet.

2 tablespoons butter, divided

2½ tablespoons extra virgin olive oil, divided

1½ cups ½-inch pieces French bread baguette

1 large onion, sliced

2 tablespoons dry white wine

2 eggs

8 cups Swiss chard or Swiss chard and red mustard, stemmed, leaves torn into 4-inch pieces

1 tablespoon red wine vinegar

Grated Parmesan cheese (optional)

MELT 1 TABLESPOON butter with 1 tablespoon olive oil in a heavy large well-seasoned cast-iron or nonstick skillet over medium-low heat. Add the baguette pieces and sauté until golden brown and toasted, about 7 minutes. Transfer the croutons to a bowl.

Melt ½ tablespoon butter with ½ tablespoon olive oil in the same skillet (no need to wash) over medium-low heat. Add the onion and sauté until browned and very tender, about 15 minutes. Add the wine and stir until it evaporates and the onions are very tender and caramelized, about 5 minutes. Push the onions to one side of the skillet. Add the remaining ½ tablespoon butter to the other side of the skillet. Crack the eggs into the skillet and fry until the whites are set on the bottom, about 1 minute. Carefully turn the eggs over and fry until the whites are set but the yolks are still runny, about 1 minute longer. Carefully transfer the eggs to a small plate.

Increase the heat to medium. Quickly add the chard to the skillet with the onions and drizzle with the remaining 1 tablespoon olive oil and the vinegar. Toss the chard until just wilted and remove from the heat. Mix in the croutons. Divide the chard mixture between 2 shallow bowls. Top the hot salad with the eggs and season with salt and pepper. Sprinkle with Parmesan, if desired, and serve.

GRILLED EGGPLANT with Heirloom Tomatoes, Fresh Mozzarella, and Pesto Vinaigrette

With this salad, I'll often grill the eggplant in the cool morning, and then assemble the salad in the evening just before serving, thus avoiding cooking in the heat of the day or barbecuing in the dark. Pair the salad with some good bread to sop up any vinaigrette that lands on your plate.

1 eggplant (about 1 pound), cut into
1/2-inch-thick rounds

Extra virgin olive oil

4 cups mixed greens

4 large heirloom tomatoes
(about 2 to 2 1/2 pounds), sliced

12 ounces fresh mozzarella, sliced into
thin rounds

Pesto Vinaigrette (page 72)

PREHEAT A GRILL or stovetop grill pan to medium heat. Brush both sides of the eggplant rounds with olive oil and sprinkle with salt and pepper. Grill the eggplant until browned and tender, turning once, about 8 minutes. Let the eggplant cool to room temperature.

Line a platter or 4 individual plates with the greens. Arrange the eggplant, tomato, and mozzarella slices attractively over the greens. Drizzle the vinaigrette over and serve.

Pesto Vinaigrette

If you have lots of fresh basil, then you should make pesto. If you have pesto, then you should make this dressing and enjoy it on sliced tomatoes, grilled vegetables, fried eggs, and freshly cooked pasta all summer long.

2/3 cup Pesto (below)

3 tablespoons extra virgin olive oil

3 tablespoons white balsamic dressing

WHISK THE INGREDIENTS to blend in a small bowl. Season the vinaigrette to taste with salt and pepper.

Pesto

Basil grows like a weed in the summer and then vanishes from even sunny climes in the winter. So I plant as much as I can in the summer and feast on pesto all season long. Yes, pesto is great over pasta, but when transformed into a bright green dressing that's drizzled over tomatoes and eggplant, who needs noodles? Pesto also freezes beautifully, so when summer-only treats like homegrown tomatoes and basil are long gone, you can enjoy this basil sauce, thinned with a little cream (about $1/3$ cup cream per cup of pesto for about 1 pound of pasta) over the aforementioned noodles.

2 cups (lightly packed) fresh basil leaves

1/2 cup pine nuts, toasted

1/2 cup grated Parmesan cheese

3 garlic cloves

1/4 cup extra virgin olive oil

COMBINE THE FIRST 4 ingredients in the bowl of a food processor. Pulse until the mixture is finely chopped. Add the olive oil and roughly purée. Season the pesto to taste with salt. *(Can be prepared ahead. Transfer the pesto to a small container and cover with plastic wrap pressed directly onto the surface of the pesto and seal tightly with a lid. Refrigerate up to 5 days or freeze up to 8 months.)*

CHOPPED SALAD with Flatbread and Labneh

Za'atar is an Arabic word for both an herb and an herb blend. The flavor is divine—herbal, musty, tart, and toasty. You can find the dried herb blend at Middle Eastern markets and some specialty stores, but I include the recipe for making the fresh version below because it is so easy and the green herbs really sing. Labneh, a rich yogurt cheese, and sumac, a ground berry with a lemony flavor, are available at Whole Foods markets and Middle Eastern markets. I buy jars of roasted sesame seeds at the supermarket, in the Asian foods section.

ZA'ATAR AND FLATBREADS

1 tablespoon minced fresh oregano

1 tablespoon roasted sesame seeds

1 tablespoon sumac

1 tablespoon minced fresh thyme

1 recipe Flatbread Dough (page 69)

Extra virgin olive oil

SALAD

2 small Persian cucumbers, sliced, or 1 large cucumber, peeled, seeded, and sliced

2 ripe tomatoes, diced

1 cup baby arugula leaves

1 tablespoon freshly squeezed lemon juice

1 tablespoon extra virgin olive oil, plus additional for drizzling

½ tablespoon coarsely chopped fresh mint leaves

½ tablespoon coarsely chopped fresh Italian parsley leaves

½ cup labneh or Greek yogurt

1 garlic clove, pressed

FOR THE ZA'ATAR and flatbreads: Preheat the oven to 450°F.

In a small bowl, combine the oregano, sesame seeds, sumac, and thyme and stir to blend.

Divide the flatbread dough into 2 even rounds. Roll out the rounds on a lightly floured surface until they measure approximately 7 inches in diameter. Lightly dust both sides of the rounds with flour. Transfer them to a heavy baking sheet. Brush the rounds generously with olive oil. Sprinkle the za'atar evenly over the olive oil and sprinkle with salt. Bake the flatbreads until golden brown, about 10 minutes.

Meanwhile, prepare the salad: Combine the cucumbers, tomatoes, arugula, lemon juice, 1 tablespoon olive oil, mint, and parsley in a medium bowl and stir to blend. Season the salad to taste with salt.

In a small bowl, stir together the labneh and garlic to blend. Spoon the labneh onto the center of 2 plates, dividing evenly. Remove the breads from the oven and transfer them to a cutting board. Using a large sharp knife or a pizza cutter, cut the flatbreads into quarters. Surround the labneh with the flatbread quarters. Spoon the salad around the labneh. Drizzle the salads with additional olive oil and serve.

FRISÉE SALAD with Goat Cheese and Roasted Grapes

I first learned to bake goat cheese from the seminal *Chez Panisse Menu Cookbook*, and it's so good that it's worth making regularly. The breaded goat cheese patties become crispy on the outside and soft and creamy on the inside when baked briefly at a high temperature. When roasted, red grapes take on a more complex, plumlike flavor. You could serve these marjoram-flecked beauties as a sophisticated dessert with lemon ice cream, but then you'd miss out on this salad. I like to use whole-wheat bread-crumbs to coat the goat cheese rounds and then serve the salad with a warm baguette.

2 cups fresh breadcrumbs (from about 4 ounces firm-textured whole grain or white bread, crusts removed)

Extra virgin olive oil

3 teaspoons chopped fresh marjoram leaves, divided

1 (8- to 11-ounce) log soft fresh goat cheese, cut into 8 rounds

2 cups (generous) red grapes

10 cups frisée

1 shallot, very thinly sliced

Honey-Marjoram Vinaigrette (page 187)

PREHEAT THE OVEN to 450°F. Spread the breadcrumbs out in a single layer on a baking sheet and toast in the oven until just golden brown, about 8 minutes. Remove from the oven and let the breadcrumbs cool on the baking sheet. (Maintain oven temperature.)

Pour a thin layer of olive oil onto a dinner plate. Place 4 goat cheese rounds in the oil and carefully turn to coat. Sprinkle the rounds with 1 teaspoon marjoram. Transfer the rounds to the breadcrumbs and turn carefully to coat the cheese with crumbs, pressing the crumbs gently onto the goat cheese rounds. Transfer the coated rounds to a heavy large rimmed baking pan. Repeat with the remaining goat cheese, marjoram, and crumbs, adding more oil to the plate if necessary. (*Goat cheese can be prepared up to 4 hours ahead; keep refrigerated.*)

Combine the grapes, 1 tablespoon olive oil, and the remaining teaspoon marjoram in a heavy skillet or roasting pan just large enough to accommodate the grapes in a single layer. Roast the grapes in the oven until the skins begin to burst and the grapes just begin to juice, about 8 minutes. Remove from the oven and let the grapes cool to room temperature. Bake the goat cheese until the crumbs are crisp and golden brown, about 5 minutes.

Combine the frisée and the shallot in a large bowl. Add enough Honey-Marjoram Vinaigrette to season to taste and coat the frisée lightly. Divide the greens among 4 plates and top with the grapes, dividing evenly. Arrange 2 warm rounds of goat cheese atop each salad. Spoon a little vinaigrette over the goat cheese, season the salads with cracked black pepper, and serve.

ROASTED TOMATO SALAD
with Arugula and Fromage Chacun à Son Goût

I make this salad a lot during the summer when I'm overrun with tomatoes. Roasting turns the tomatoes into rich, meaty morsels that are heavenly paired with cheese. *Chacun à son goût* means "to each his own taste." In this recipe, it's to each his own . . . *cheese.* In my family, everyone customizes the tomato topping to their taste: My husband, Martin, likes the tomatoes hot, capped with Idiazabal (smoked sheep's milk cheese from Spain); my daughter Theresa prefers them warm with goat cheese crumbles; and my daughter Celeste likes the tomatoes served room temperature with a thick blanket of burrata (cream-filled fresh mozzarella). It's all good to me, as I love the tomatoes every and any way, even served up straight with no cheese at all, especially with some toasted or grilled rustic bread.

ROASTED TOMATOES

3 tablespoons extra virgin olive oil, plus more for brushing

2 pounds small or plum tomatoes (about 2 inches in diameter), halved lengthwise

4 garlic cloves, chopped

1 teaspoon herbes de Provence

1/2 teaspoon kosher salt

8 ounces cheese, such as grated Idiazabal cheese (about 1 cup), soft, fresh goat cheese, or burrata*

SALAD

6 tablespoons extra virgin olive oil

2 tablespoons red wine vinegar

2 garlic cloves, pressed

1/2 teaspoon kosher salt

12 cups arugula

FOR THE ROASTED tomatoes: Preheat the oven to 375°F. Brush a heavy rimmed baking sheet with olive oil. Arrange the tomatoes, cut side up, on the prepared baking sheet. Drizzle with the 3 tablespoons olive oil and sprinkle with the garlic, herbes de Provence, and salt. Roast the tomatoes in the oven until soft and beginning to turn brown, about 50 minutes. Turn off the oven. Top the tomatoes with cheese, and return to the oven and let stand until the cheese melts, about 4 minutes. Remove from the oven and let the tomatoes cool slightly, on the baking sheet until they are warm.

Meanwhile, prepare the salad: Whisk the olive oil, vinegar, garlic, and salt to blend in a large bowl. Add the arugula and toss to coat. Divide the arugula among 6 plates. Top the greens with the tomatoes, dividing evenly, and serve.

*If using burrata, allow the tomatoes to cool to room temperature before topping with cheese.

FREEKEH SALAD
with Apricots, Grilled Halloumi, and Zucchini

Freekeh, a tasty Levantine grain, is made from green wheat that is sun dried and toasted by burning the chaff. The toasty flavor pairs nicely with grilled zucchini and salty halloumi cheese. Halloumi, a firm grilling and frying cheese from Cyprus, can be purchased, along with the freekeh, at a Middle Eastern market, but it's also turning up at more and more specialty markets and even supermarkets. If you prefer, crumbled feta cheese makes a nice substitution. When fresh apricots are not in season, use thinly sliced dried apricots instead.

4 tablespoons extra virgin olive oil, divided, plus additional for brushing

2 cups freekeh

$1/2$ teaspoon kosher salt

$1\frac{1}{4}$ pounds zucchini (about 3 or 4), cut lengthwise into quarters

$1/2$ teaspoon cumin seed

$1/4$ teaspoon ground cinnamon

1 (8.8-ounce) package halloumi cheese, cut into $1/2$-inch-thick slices

$1/3$ cup white balsamic vinegar

1 garlic clove, pressed

4 firm-ripe apricots, pitted and sliced

$3/4$ cup chopped green onions

$1/2$ cup chopped toasted almonds or pistachios

$1/2$ cup chopped fresh Italian parsley leaves

HEAT 2 TABLESPOONS olive oil in a heavy large saucepan over medium-high heat. Add the freekeh and stir until the grains are coated with olive oil and lightly toasted, about 4 minutes. Add $3\frac{1}{2}$ cups water and $1/2$ teaspoon kosher salt and reduce the heat to medium. Simmer until water is level with the freekeh and holes appear in the center of the cooking grain, about 10 minutes. Cover and simmer over low heat until all the water is absorbed and the freekeh is tender, about 10 minutes. Transfer the freekeh to a large bowl and fluff with a fork.

Prepare a grill to medium-high heat or heat a stovetop grill pan over medium-high heat. Brush all sides of the zucchini with olive oil and sprinkle with the cumin seed, cinnamon, and some kosher salt. Brush the halloumi generously with olive oil. Grill the zucchini and halloumi until the zucchini is well browned on all sides and tender, turning occasionally, and the halloumi is browned on both sides, turning once, about 8 minutes. Transfer to a plate and let cool slightly.

In a small bowl, whisk the remaining 2 tablespoons olive oil with the vinegar and garlic to blend. Add the dressing to the freekeh along with the apricots, green onions, almonds, and parsley. Cut the zucchini and the halloumi into $1/2$-inch pieces and add to the salad. Mix briefly to combine and serve. *(The salad can be prepared 1 day ahead; cover and refrigerate.)*

SALADS with Fish and Seafood

Seared Salmon with Quinoa, Asparagus, Sorrel, and Lemon Spinach

Lemon Vinaigrette

Sardine-Stuffed Piquillo Peppers with Lemony Greens and Whole-Wheat Croutons

Preserved Lemons

Singapore-Style Chinese New Year Raw Fish "Tossed" Salad

Fried Wonton Strips

White Anchovy, Potato, and Parsley Salad

Lobster Salad with Watermelon, Yellow Tomato, Mâche, and Mint

Salade Niçoise un Peu Classique

Anchovy Vinaigrette

Hardboiled Eggs

Smoked Salmon, Asparagus, and Watercress Salad with Sour Cream Dill Sauce

Baby Octopus and White Bean Salad

Fennel, Roasted Beet, and Smoked Whitefish Salad with Horseradish Cream

Horseradish Cream

Seafood-Stuffed Avocado Salad

Grilled Baby Artichoke and Asparagus Salad with Shrimp and Saffron Aioli

Saffron Aioli

Mexican Beach Ceviche with Avocado

Spinach Salad with Grilled Shrimp and Peppers

Paella Salad

OPPOSITE: Romaine Rouge d'Hiver Lettuce

A LITTLE FISH WITH BIG FLAVOR

Anchovies are both revered and reviled. I can think of no other food that is scorned in concept, but enjoyed heartily in so many popular dishes. People who claim to hate anchovies unknowingly savor the common and abundant little fish in various guises—including soups, stir-fries, sauces, and salads. Anchovies first swam their way to my heart in a Caesar Salad. The salad was made tableside, and I can still picture the white-jacketed waiter artfully crushing the glistening fillets against the side of the large wooden bowl with a silver fork. I'm sure that for many the Caesar serves as the anchovy "gateway" dish.

Anchovies school in warm oceans all over the world, but perhaps where they serve as the most ubiquitous yet subversive flavor agent is in Southeast Asia. Experienced cooks know that it's difficult to make authentic tasting Thai or Vietnamese food without fish sauce—try to substitute soy sauce and your finished dish will lack depth. Fish sauce is not only made from anchovies, it's made from anchovies that are fermented to a fragrant point of liquidation. This fact would surely surprise many who claim an aversion to the little fish, but love Pad Thai and Pho—traditional dishes of which fish sauce is an essential component. Anchovies in some form or another are featured in several of my recipes. The small, silver powerhouse adds zip, zest, salt, a little funk, and lots of umami to dressings, vinaigrettes, and salads. They will please anchovy enthusiasts and skeptics alike.

SEARED SALMON
with Quinoa, Asparagus, Sorrel, and Lemon Spinach

Quickly seared salmon sits atop a bed of lemon-dressed quinoa and spinach. Sorrel is a tender, large-leafed herb with a tart, lemony flavor. Sorrel is sold at herb stands at farmers' markets. If sorrel is unavailable, you can still enjoy the salad without it. Nasturtiums bloom in my garden when the sorrel is at its peak—I like to throw a few of the bright yellow, orange, and red petals into the mix, too.

1 bunch asparagus (about 1 pound), trimmed

2 garlic cloves, minced

1/2 teaspoon kosher salt

1 cup quinoa

Lemon Vinaigrette (opposite)

1 cup finely sliced sorrel leaves

4 green onions, sliced

8 cups baby spinach leaves

1 tablespoon extra virgin olive oil

4 (5-ounce) pieces skinless salmon fillet (about 3/4 inch thick)

Lemon wedges

Nasturtium petals (optional)

FILL A LARGE skillet with 1 inch of salted water and bring to a simmer over high heat. Add the asparagus, and cover and cook until crisp-tender, about 2 minutes. Using tongs, transfer the asparagus to a bowl of ice water to cool. Drain the asparagus and pat dry with a clean dish towel. Cut the asparagus on a diagonal into 1-inch pieces. *(Asparagus can be prepared 1 day ahead. Cover and refrigerate.)*

Bring 2 1/2 cups water, garlic, and the 1/2 teaspoon salt to a simmer in a medium saucepan over medium heat. Add the quinoa and bring to a simmer. Continue simmering until the liquid is reduced by half, about 10 minutes. Reduce the heat to low, cover, and cook until the quinoa is tender and the liquid is absorbed, about 10 minutes. Remove from the heat, uncover, and let cool slightly. Stir 1/4 cup of the Lemon Vinaigrette into the quinoa and cool completely. Stir in the sorrel, green onions, and asparagus and season to taste with salt and pepper. *(Quinoa can be prepared 4 hours ahead; cover and keep at cool room temperature.)*

Toss the spinach with half of the remaining vinaigrette. Divide the spinach among 4 plates and top with the quinoa, dividing evenly.

Heat the olive oil in a very large, heavy skillet over high heat. Season both sides of the salmon with salt and pepper. Add the salmon to the skillet and cook until just browned on the bottom, about 2 minutes. Turn the salmon and quickly sear until the second sides are just golden brown and the salmon is not quite opaque in center, about 2 minutes longer. Top the quinoa with the hot salmon. Drizzle the salmon with the remaining vinaigrette. Garnish the salads with lemon wedges, scatter nasturtium petals over the salads, if using, and serve.

Lemon Vinaigrette

So simple yet so brightly flavored, this tart dressing is great on fish and vegetables alike.

6 tablespoons extra virgin olive oil

3 tablespoons freshly squeezed lemon juice

2 tablespoons white balsamic vinegar

½ teaspoon kosher salt

½ teaspoon grated lemon peel

WHISK ALL THE ingredients to blend in a small bowl. *(Dressing can be made 1 week ahead. Cover the dressing and refrigerate, allowing it to return to room temperature before using.)*

SARDINE-STUFFED PIQUILLO PEPPERS
with Lemony Greens and Whole-Wheat Croutons

This salad comes together quickly with cool pantry staples. I've served this light meal to friends who claim they don't like sardines, and they find it delicious. Piquillo peppers are deep red, pointy peppers that are packaged in jars (*piquillo* means "little beak" in Spanish). I like to make my own preserved lemons, but you can purchase those jarred as well.

2 (3.75-ounce) tins boneless, skinless sardines in olive oil, drained

1½ tablespoons finely chopped preserved lemon (below), divided

2 teaspoons minced fresh oregano or 1 teaspoon dried, crumbled

10 piquillo peppers from a jar, drained

2 tablespoons extra virgin olive oil

2 tablespoons freshly squeezed lemon juice

1 garlic clove, pressed

½ teaspoon kosher salt

6 cups mixed greens, such as arugula and romaine

¼ cup very thinly sliced sweet onion, such as Vidalia

1 tablespoon capers, drained

Whole-Wheat Croutons (page 146)

IN A SMALL bowl, gently stir the sardines, 1 tablespoon preserved lemon, and the oregano to blend, breaking the sardines into smaller pieces. Season the sardine mixture with freshly ground black pepper. Hold the peppers with the opening facing upward and stuff with the sardine mixture, dividing evenly.

In another small bowl, whisk the olive oil, lemon juice, garlic, salt, and the remaining ½ tablespoon preserved lemon to blend. In a medium bowl, toss the greens and onion slices with 1 tablespoon of the dressing. Divide the salad between 2 salad plates. Top the salads with the stuffed peppers and sprinkle with capers, dividing evenly. Season the salads with freshly ground black pepper and top with the croutons. Drizzle the remaining dressing over the salads and serve.

Preserved Lemons

I always make a batch of preserved lemons when my Meyer lemon tree fruits in the winter. Meyer lemons have thin skins with highly perfumed essential oils. They are super juicy and are less acidic than Eureka lemons, which are the familiar supermarket variety. While Meyer lemons are preferred for preserving, if you have a Eureka lemon tree, you can use those lemons. Four or six jars (a double or triple recipe) usually lasts throughout the year, until the following crop of lemons is ripe. After removing the desired amount of preserved lemons from the jar, be sure that the remaining lemons are completely covered with olive oil—you may need to add a touch more.

3 or 4 Meyer lemons	**Extra virgin olive oil**
4 tablespoons (about) kosher salt	

WASH AND DRY the lemons and cut lengthwise into quarters. Place 1 lemon quarter into each of two 8-ounce jars. Sprinkle the lemon with some of the salt. Repeat, nestling enough lemon quarters into each jar to fill it completely, pressing gently on the lemons and sprinkling with salt between each addition. Pour enough olive oil over the top of the lemons to cover them by ¹/₂ inch. Seal the jars and refrigerate at least one week before using. *(Preserved lemons can be made several months ahead. Keep lemons refrigerated, making sure lemons are completely submerged in lemon juice and olive oil.)*

SINGAPORE-STYLE CHINESE NEW YEAR RAW FISH "TOSSED" SALAD

My friend Rachel, who grew up in Singapore, introduced me to this unique salad and fun New Year's tradition. Raw fish, fruit, and vegetables are artfully arranged in a bowl, dressed with a plum-sauce dressing, and sprinkled with peanuts. Once the salad is presented, guests participate in "tossing" it with chopsticks, the object being to fling the salad as high as they can to ensure good luck in the year to come. Fried wonton crisps are said to symbolize gold, and they add a fun crunch to the salad, but they can be omitted if you are looking to save on calories. The best place to find good-quality raw fish is the sushi stand in specialty markets, where they will expertly slice the fish for you.

DRESSING

¼ cup freshly squeezed lime juice

2 tablespoons toasted sesame oil

2 tablespoons plum sauce

2 teaspoons grated peeled fresh ginger

2 small cloves garlic, minced

SALAD

1 pink grapefruit

1 ripe mango

1 medium carrot, peeled and cut into fine julienne

1 (8-ounce) piece jicama, peeled and cut into fine julienne

1 small red bell pepper, stemmed, seeded, and cut into fine julienne

8 ounces assorted raw fish, such as albacore, salmon, and halibut, thinly sliced into 1x2-inch pieces

Sea salt

4 green onions, thinly sliced on a diagonal

¼ cup chopped fresh cilantro

¼ cup chopped salted roasted peanuts

Fried Wonton Strips (page 90; optional)

FOR THE DRESSING: Whisk all the ingredients to blend in a small bowl.

For the salad: Peel the grapefruit and separate the pieces into sections. Remove the pith and membrane from the sections and, using your fingertips, crumble the pulp into small bits into the center of a large shallow bowl.

Using a small sharp knife, peel the mango. Set the mango on the cutting surface, narrow side on the surface. Using a large sharp knife, cut off the lobes of fruit along both sides of the seed. Place the seed on the cutting surface, flat-side down, and cut remaining fruit off the seed. Cut the mango fruit into julienne slices. Arrange the mango along the side of the grapefruit. Arrange the carrot, jicama, and red pepper around the grapefruit, leaving space for the fish. *(The dressing and the salad can be prepared several hours ahead. Cover them separately and refrigerate up to 6 hours.)*

Fan the sliced fish alongside the vegetables. Sprinkle the salad with sea salt. Top the grapefruit with the green onions and cilantro, and sprinkle with the peanuts.

At the table, pour the dressing over the salad. Allow diners to toss the salad with chopsticks. Serve the salad, passing the fried wonton strips separately.

Fried Wonton Strips

| MAKES ABOUT 2 CUPS

Wonton wrappers are available in the refrigerated section of most supermarkets and at Asian markets. Unused uncooked wonton wrappers can be frozen for future use.

Roasted peanut oil

8 wonton wrappers, sliced into
1/2-inch-wide strips

HEAT 1 INCH of oil in a heavy medium deep skillet over medium-high heat until very hot. Add half of the wonton strips and fry until golden brown on both sides, about 1 minute. Using a slotted spoon, transfer the strips to paper towels or a brown paper bag to drain. Repeat with the remaining strips. *(Fried wonton strips can be made 1 day ahead. Let cool and store in an airtight container at room temperature.)*

WHITE ANCHOVY, POTATO, AND PARSLEY SALAD

White anchovies, sometimes labeled *bocquerones*, are anchovy fillets that are marinated in oil and vinegar, making them taste lightly pickled. Unlike canned anchovies, white anchovies have a delicate flavor and tender texture. Look for them in the refrigerated section at specialty foods stores or online.

1 pound small red-skinned potatoes

1 cup fresh Italian parsley leaves

2 tablespoons plus 4 teaspoons extra virgin olive oil, divided

6 teaspoons white wine vinegar, divided

3 garlic cloves, pressed, divided

Sea salt

½ red onion, very thinly sliced

4 celery ribs, trimmed and thinly sliced

24 white anchovy fillets from about one 7.1-ounce package (200 grams)

4 hardboiled eggs (page 97), sliced into rounds

BOIL THE POTATOES in rapidly boiling salted water until just tender when pierced with a thin knife or skewer, about 10 minutes. Drain the potatoes and let cool completely. *(Potatoes can be cooked 2 days ahead. Cover and refrigerate.)*

In a small bowl, combine the parsley leaves with 4 teaspoons olive oil, 4 teaspoons vinegar, 1 garlic clove, and a pinch of sea salt and let stand while preparing salad ingredients, about 10 minutes.

Slice the potatoes into rounds. Arrange the dressed parsley attractively over 4 dinner plates, dividing evenly. Place the potato slices atop the parsley, then top with the red onion and the celery. Arrange the anchovy fillets over the vegetables, dividing evenly. Top the salads with hardboiled eggs.

Whisk the remaining 2 tablespoons olive oil, 2 teaspoons vinegar and 2 garlic cloves to blend in a small bowl. Sprinkle the salads with sea salt and season with freshly ground black pepper. Drizzle each salad with the dressing and serve.

LOBSTER SALAD
with Watermelon, Yellow Tomato, Mâche, and Mint

Lobster is very rich; pairing it with the bright, clear flavors of watermelon, mint, and yellow tomatoes is perfection. Serve this refreshing, fancy salad for a summer celebration dinner with a chilled sparkler. If you are not up for cooking your own lobster, a good fishmonger will cook it for you, or you can purchase cooked lobster tails. About half of one of those sweet mini watermelons is just the right amount for this salad.

DRESSING

2 tablespoons freshly squeezed lime juice

2 tablespoons mayonnaise

1 tablespoon extra virgin olive oil

1 garlic clove, pressed

$1/2$ teaspoon sugar

$1/4$ teaspoon kosher salt

SALAD

2 cooked lobsters* (about $1 1/4$ pounds each) or 2 large cooked lobster tails, chilled

2 cups mâche rosettes or baby arugula leaves

2 cups ($3/4$-inch) cubes chilled watermelon

1 large yellow (preferably) heirloom tomato, cored and cut into $3/4$-inch cubes or 8 yellow pear tomatoes, cut in half

$1/2$ Persian cucumber, peeled, quartered, and thinly sliced

2 green onions, thinly sliced

2 tablespoons fresh mint leaves

1 small jalapeño pepper, stemmed, seeded, and finely diced

FOR THE DRESSING: Whisk all the ingredients to blend in a small bowl. *(The dressing can be prepared up to 2 days ahead; cover and refrigerate.)*

For the salad: If using whole cooked lobsters, break off the head and body sections from the tail with your hands. Break off the large claws. (Discard the head and body sections or reserve for making stock.) With a lobster-cracking tool, crack the claws and remove the meat. Using kitchen shears, cut the shell down the center of the tail section on the top and bottom sides. Remove the meat from the tail and cut crosswise into thin slices. *(Lobster can be prepared 1 day ahead. Cover in plastic and refrigerate.)*

In a large bowl, combine the mâche, watermelon, tomatoes, cucumber, green onions, mint leaves, and jalapeño. Add the lobster and the dressing and toss just to combine. Serve immediately.

*To cook lobster: Bring a very large pot of salted water to a boil. Using tongs, carefully add the lobsters to the pot, head first. Partially cover the pot and simmer 8 minutes. Remove the lobsters from the water and let cool completely. *(Lobsters can be boiled 1 day ahead. Drain and refrigerate.)*

SALADE NIÇOISE UN PEU CLASSIQUE

A true salade niçoise should feature only raw vegetables. My version is not completely authentic as I dress this "a little bit classic" version with bold anchovy vinaigrette. Thinly sliced basil leaves, called chiffonade, are easy to make: Simply stack the leaves neatly and roll into a cylinder. Using a sharp knife, thinly slice the cylinder crosswise into thin strips. Serve the salad with thinly sliced pain rustique.

12 cups mixed greens

2 (5-ounce) cans tuna packed in olive oil, drained

1 red bell pepper, stemmed, seeded, and thinly sliced

1 small (pickling or Persian) cucumber, halved and sliced

2 celery ribs, thinly sliced

4 green onions, thinly sliced

8 leaves fresh basil, thinly sliced (chiffonade), or ¼ cup fresh Italian parsley leaves

4 small ripe tomatoes, each cut into 6 wedges

5 artichoke hearts with stems (from a 14.6-ounce jar), cut lengthwise into quarters

4 hardboiled eggs (page 97), peeled and quartered

32 pitted niçoise olives or 20 pitted kalamata olives, cut in half

Anchovy Vinaigrette (below)

DIVIDE THE MIXED greens among 4 plates, creating attractive beds. Scatter the tuna, red pepper, cucumber, celery, green onions, and basil over the lettuce, dividing evenly. Arrange the tomatoes, artichokes, eggs, and olives attractively atop the salads, dividing evenly. Serve the salads, allowing diners to spoon dressing over their own salads.

Anchovy Vinaigrette

This dressing makes a great dip for crudités. For ease and quick cleanup, chop the anchovies on a thin, pliable plastic cutting board (usually used for raw chicken).

2 (2-ounce) cans anchovies in olive oil, drained (about 16 fillets), finely chopped

¼ cup red wine vinegar

2 teaspoons Dijon mustard

4 garlic cloves, pressed

½ cup extra virgin olive oil

STIR THE ANCHOVIES, vinegar, mustard, and garlic to blend in a medium bowl. Whisk in the olive oil. Season the dressing with freshly ground black pepper. (*Vinaigrette can be prepared 3 days ahead; cover and refrigerate.*)

SMOKED SALMON, ASPARAGUS, AND WATERCRESS SALAD with Sour Cream Dill Sauce

This salad makes a nice brunch dish for a spring party. Baby spinach is a good stand-in for the watercress. If desired, serve the salad with Swedish rye bread.

½ cup sour cream

2 tablespoons freshly squeezed lemon juice

2 tablespoons extra virgin olive oil

2 tablespoons minced fresh dill

1 tablespoon Dijon mustard

½ teaspoon grated lemon peel

1 bunch asparagus, trimmed

2 bunches watercress, trimmed (about 8 cups)

2 Persian cucumbers or 1 peeled cucumber, thinly sliced

4 ounces thinly sliced smoked salmon

2 green onions, thinly sliced

4 hardboiled eggs (below), peeled and quartered

IN A SMALL bowl, combine the first 6 ingredients and stir to blend for the dressing. *(Dressing can be prepared up to 3 days ahead; cover and refrigerate.)*

Bring a large skillet with 1 inch of salted water to simmer over high heat. Add the asparagus, and cover and cook until crisp-tender, about 2 minutes. Using tongs, transfer the asparagus to a bowl of ice water to cool. Drain the asparagus and pat dry with a clean dish towel. Cut the asparagus into 2- to 3-inch pieces on a diagonal. *(Asparagus can be prepared 1 day ahead. Cover and refrigerate.)*

Divide the watercress among 4 individual salad bowls or plates. Top with the asparagus, cucumber, salmon, and green onions. Garnish the salads with the egg quarters and serve with the dressing.

Hardboiled Eggs

It's always good to have a few hardboiled eggs on hand, as they make a great addition to any number of salads and a quick and healthy snack.

4 large or extra-large eggs

COVER THE EGGS with water in a small saucepan and bring to a gentle simmer over medium heat. Simmer the eggs slowly for 5 minutes. Remove the pan from the heat; cover and let stand 5 minutes. Rinse the eggs with cold water to cool. Refrigerate the eggs until well chilled. *(Eggs can be hardboiled up to 1 week ahead; cover and refrigerate.)*

BABY OCTOPUS AND WHITE BEAN SALAD

You can make this salad with fresh, frozen, or prepared baby octopus. Fresh or frozen baby octopus is available at some fish markets—I buy mine at Seafood City, the Filipino market a few blocks from my home. Or you can use octopus from a marinated octopus salad, available at Italian delis and specialty foods stores. If you have never tasted octopus, don't be afraid. While it may look bizarre, it is tender, chewy, and mild flavored. If it still proves too elusive or exotic, this salad is also good when made with two cans of drained tuna. Serve the salad in shallow bowls with whole-wheat French bread alongside and chilled white wine.

8 ounces baby octopus, thawed if frozen, or 14 to 15 ounces (about 2 packages) marinated baby octopus salad, drained

2 bay leaves, preferably fresh (for fresh or frozen octopus)

1/2 teaspoon kosher salt (for fresh or frozen octopus)

6 tablespoons extra virgin olive oil

1/4 cup freshly squeezed lemon juice

3 garlic cloves, pressed or minced

2 (15-ounce) cans cannellini beans, rinsed and drained

1 fennel bulb, trimmed and chopped

4 celery ribs, sliced

1/2 red onion, thinly sliced

2/3 cup chopped fresh Italian parsley

IF USING FRESH or frozen thawed octopus: Combine the octopus, bay leaves, and salt in a heavy large pot. Add enough water to cover by several inches and bring to a boil. Reduce the heat to a simmer and add salt. Simmer until the octopus is very tender when pierced with a sharp knife, about 1 to 1 1/2 hours. Drain and let cool completely.

Thinly slice the cooked or the marinated octopus heads and cut the tentacle sections in half if large.

In a large bowl, whisk the oil, lemon juice, and garlic to blend. Add the octopus along with the remaining ingredients and stir to combine. *(The salad can be prepared 1 day ahead; cover and refrigerate. Before serving, adjust the seasoning, adding additional lemon juice or olive oil if necessary.)*

FENNEL, ROASTED BEET, AND SMOKED WHITEFISH SALAD with Horseradish Cream

Smoked whitefish or smoked trout are both excellent in this salad. Look for smoked whitefish at delis and smoked trout in places where trout fishing is popular. Thinly sliced multigrain toasts spread with unsalted butter and sprinkled with sea salt make an excellent accompaniment.

8 cups mixed greens

4 roasted beets (page 56), peeled and thinly sliced

1 small fennel bulb, trimmed and shaved or cut into thin slices

½ small white onion, shaved or cut into thin slices

6 ounces flaked, skinned, boned smoked whitefish or trout (from about 8 ounces)

Horseradish Cream (below)

DIVIDE THE GREENS among 4 plates. Top the greens with the beets, fennel, and onion slices, dividing evenly. Scatter the fish over the salads. Spoon the dressing over and serve.

Horseradish Cream

Horseradish and sour cream make for a delightful, cool burn. Try the dressing on toast or a bagel with smoked fish.

½ cup sour cream

1 tablespoon freshly squeezed lemon juice

½ teaspoon kosher salt

4 to 6 tablespoons prepared horseradish

STIR THE SOUR cream, lemon juice, and salt to blend in a small bowl. Stir in enough horseradish to season to taste. Season the cream generously with freshly ground black pepper. *(Horseradish Cream can be made 3 days ahead. Cover and refrigerate.)*

SEAFOOD-STUFFED AVOCADO SALAD

This salad conjures images of country club fare and ladies who lunch. Elegant and slightly old-fashioned in its presentation, it's still a charmer—even for men and career women. Pass a basket of sliced baguette and chilled butter pats at the table.

DRESSING

2 tablespoons freshly squeezed lemon juice

1 tablespoon chopped fresh tarragon

1½ teaspoons Dijon mustard

1 garlic clove, pressed

¼ teaspoon kosher salt

6 tablespoons extra virgin olive oil

SALAD

8 ounces cooked best-quality lump crabmeat, such as Dungeness or blue crab

8 ounces cooked large shrimp

2 green onions, thinly sliced

1 head butter lettuce, separated into leaves

2 ripe large avocados, halved, peeled, and pitted

Additional fresh tarragon leaves

FOR THE DRESSING: Whisk the lemon juice, tarragon, mustard, garlic, and salt to blend in a small bowl. Gradually whisk in the olive oil.

For the salad: Combine the crabmeat, shrimp, and green onions in a medium bowl. Add 2 tablespoons dressing to the seafood salad and stir gently. Season the salad to taste with salt and pepper. *(Can be prepared 1 day ahead. Cover and chill.)*

Line 4 plates with the butter lettuce leaves. Top each with an avocado half. Fill the avocados with the salad, dividing evenly. Drizzle the remaining dressing over the greens and sprinkle with the tarragon leaves.

GRILLED BABY ARTICHOKE AND ASPARAGUS
SALAD with Shrimp and Saffron Aioli

If baby artichokes are not available, go ahead and use larger ones, as you wouldn't want to miss out on this heavenly dish. To prepare full-size artichokes to use in this recipe, simply cook two or three larger artichokes in boiling salted water for about 25 minutes until almost tender. Cool and quarter the artichokes, then remove the chokes and trim away the tough leaves. Now you are ready to grill them as directed below—you just won't be able to eat the entire artichoke as you would with the tender young ones. Grilled slices of rustic bread taste great slathered with the aioli, too.

2 tablespoons plus 2 teaspoons extra virgin olive oil, plus more for brushing

2 garlic cloves, pressed

1 teaspoon paprika

1 teaspoon grated lemon peel

1/4 teaspoon crushed red pepper

1 1/2 pounds shrimp, peeled and deveined

12 baby artichokes

1 bunch asparagus, trimmed

6 cups arugula

1 lemon, cut into wedges

Saffron Aioli (page 104)

IN A LARGE bowl, combine 2 tablespoons olive oil, garlic, paprika, lemon peel, and crushed red pepper. Add the shrimp and toss to coat. Cover and refrigerate 2 to 8 hours.

Prepare a grill to medium heat. Peel back the outer leaves of the artichokes until the remaining leaves are a pale yellow-green. Cut off the tip of each artichoke and trim the stems. Cut the artichokes in half lengthwise and transfer to a large rimmed baking sheet. Brush the artichokes with olive oil. Add the asparagus to the baking sheet with the artichokes and brush with olive oil.

Line a large platter with the arugula. Drizzle the arugula with the remaining 2 teaspoons olive oil. Squeeze some lemon over the arugula, about 2 teaspoons. Arrange the shrimp, then the artichokes, and then the asparagus on the grill. Sprinkle the shrimp and the vegetables with salt and grill, turning, until shrimp are cooked through and the artichokes and asparagus are tender and browned in spots, about 6 or 7 minutes. Arrange the shrimp, artichokes, and asparagus atop the arugula. Garnish with the lemon wedges and serve with the Saffron Aioli.

Saffron Aioli

Aioli is a garlic-and-olive-oil condiment popular in the Provence region of France. Adding a little saffron makes it an especially good accompaniment to grilled fish and vegetables.

Small pinch saffron threads

¼ cup mayonnaise (preferably organic)

1 egg yolk

3 garlic cloves, pressed

⅔ cup extra virgin olive oil

1 tablespoon freshly squeezed lemon juice

½ teaspoon kosher salt

HEAT THE SAFFRON threads in a heavy small saucepan over medium heat until just fragrant (do not burn), about 20 seconds. Remove the pan from the heat and add 1 tablespoon water. Cover the pan and steep the saffron until the water is dark orange, about 5 minutes.

In a deep bowl, whisk the mayonnaise, egg yolk, garlic, and saffron mixture to blend. Drizzle about 2 teaspoons of the olive oil over the saffron mixture in the bowl and whisk vigorously, about 30 seconds. Repeat twice more, adding 2 teaspoons oil and whisking. Slowly add the remaining olive oil to the saffron mixture, pouring it into the bowl in a slow, steady stream while whisking constantly, continuing to whisk until the aioli thickens to a spreadable consistency. Whisk in the lemon juice and salt and season with black pepper. *(Aioli can be prepared 1 week ahead; cover and refrigerate.)*

MEXICAN BEACH CEVICHE WITH AVOCADO

Start with warm ocean waves, a fine-sand beach, and a palm palapa, then add an ice-cold beer with lime and a fresh seafood ceviche salad that is crisp, tart, creamy with avocado, and crunchy with tortilla chips. For me, this is heaven. When I can't enjoy the location, I indulge in the food and drink. This little taste of tropical paradise can be eaten soon after making, or it can marinate overnight in the refrigerator.

12 ounces fresh tilapia fillet (preferably American farmed), cut into 1/2-inch pieces

12 ounces bay scallops, halved

1 1/4 cups (about) freshly squeezed lime juice

1 teaspoon (about) kosher salt, divided

1/4 cup ketchup

1/4 cup extra virgin olive oil

4 garlic cloves, pressed

4 cups chopped tomatoes

1 cup chopped white onion

3/4 cup chopped fresh cilantro

2 jalapeño peppers, stemmed, seeded, and minced

12 romaine heart lettuce leaves

3 large avocados, peeled, pitted, and diced

Tortilla Strips (page 48)

Lime wedges

Hot pepper sauce, such as Valentina or Tapatío (optional)

COMBINE THE TILAPIA and the scallops in a large, nonreactive bowl. Add enough lime juice to cover the fish. Stir in 1/2 teaspoon kosher salt. Refrigerate the fish for 1 hour, allowing the lime juice to "cook" the fish.

In another large bowl, combine the ketchup, olive oil, garlic, and the remaining 1/2 teaspoon salt and stir to blend. Remove 1/4 cup of the lime juice mixture from the fish and stir it into the ketchup mixture. Using a slotted spoon, transfer the fish mixture to the large bowl along with the tomatoes, onion, cilantro, and jalapeños. *(Ceviche can be made 1 day ahead; cover and refrigerate.)*

Arrange 3 romaine leaves like spokes in each of 4 shallow bowls. Add the avocado to the ceviche, stirring gently to combine. Season the ceviche to taste with additional salt if necessary. Spoon the ceviche over the romaine leaves on each plate, dividing evenly. Garnish the salad with tortilla strips and lime wedges and serve, passing hot pepper sauce if desired.

SPINACH SALAD with Grilled Shrimp and Peppers

Grilled peppers of any kind make an excellent addition to this salad—I especially like the very cute and colorful mini peppers that are available at most supermarkets.

1 pound large shrimp, peeled and deveined

2 tablespoons extra virgin olive oil

2 garlic cloves, pressed

8 ounces mixed mini bell peppers

8 cups baby spinach leaves

2 cups cherry tomatoes, cut in half

2 Persian cucumbers, sliced into rounds

½ small red onion, thinly sliced

Mediterranean Lemon Dressing (page 196)

Feta cheese, crumbled

2 tablespoons fresh oregano leaves

Lemon wedges

Pita Crisps (see Garlic Naan Crisps, page 119) or pita bread

COMBINE THE SHRIMP, olive oil, and garlic in a bowl. Cover and chill 1 hour or overnight.

Prepare a grill to medium-high heat. Add the peppers to the shrimp and stir to coat with olive oil. Grill the shrimp and peppers until browned and tender, turning once or twice, about 6 minutes. Transfer the shrimp and peppers to a plate.

In a very large bowl, combine the spinach, tomatoes, cucumbers, and red onion with the Mediterranean Lemon Dressing and toss to coat. Add the warm shrimp and peppers and toss lightly. Divide the salad among plates. Sprinkle the salads with feta cheese and oregano leaves. Garnish the salads with lemon wedges and Pita Crisps and serve.

PAELLA SALAD

Orzo, a small rice-shaped pasta, stands in for the paella rice in this salad adaptation of the Spanish favorite. Smoked paprika (the finest is *pimentón de la Vera*), hails from eastern Spain. The robustly flavored spice, ground from smoke-dried peppers, is available in *dulce* (sweet) or *picante* (hot) varieties. Both work beautifully in this salad, which can be served room temperature or chilled. If you've got to have your greens, you can serve the paella mix on a bed of crisp romaine or arugula leaves.

4 tablespoons extra virgin olive oil, divided

8 ounces orzo pasta (about 1¼ cups)

4 garlic cloves, minced

⅛ teaspoon saffron threads

2¾ cups chicken broth

½ cup frozen peas

8 ounces peeled, deveined shrimp, cut into ½-inch pieces

1 teaspoon smoked paprika

1 small red bell pepper, diced

1 cup halved small cherry tomatoes

2 ounces diced Spanish dry-cured chorizo (about ½ cup)

⅓ cup thinly sliced green onions

2 tablespoons chopped fresh Italian parsley

2 tablespoons sherry vinegar

HEAT 1 TABLESPOON of the olive oil in a heavy medium saucepan over medium heat. Add the orzo and stir until golden brown, about 3 minutes. Add the garlic and saffron and stir until fragrant, about 30 seconds. Pour in the broth and bring to a boil. Reduce the heat to low and simmer until the orzo is tender and the broth is completely absorbed, about 12 minutes. Transfer the orzo to a large bowl and stir in the peas and 1 tablespoon of the olive oil. Cool completely.

Meanwhile, heat 1 tablespoon olive oil in a heavy medium skillet over high heat. Add the shrimp pieces and sprinkle with the paprika and a little kosher salt. Stir-fry until the shrimp is opaque, about 2 minutes. Remove from the heat and let cool slightly. Stir the shrimp and all the oil and spices from the pan into the orzo, breaking up the pasta as you stir it. Stir in the red pepper, tomatoes, chorizo, green onions, and parsley. Drizzle 2 tablespoons sherry vinegar and 1 tablespoon olive oil over all. Season the salad with freshly ground black pepper and stir to combine. *(The salad can be prepared 1 day ahead. Cover and refrigerate. Stir the salad before serving, adding the remaining 1 tablespoon of olive oil and sherry vinegar if necessary.)*

SALADS with Poultry

Chinese-Style Chicken Salad with Tangerines

Indonesian Slaw with Pineapple, Chicken, and Spicy Peanut Dressing

Curried Chicken on Baby Spinach with Mango Chutney Dressing and Garlic Naan Crisps

Garlic Naan Crisps

Roast Chicken Breasts

Red Mustard and Bread Salad with Roast Chicken

Cobb Salad

Jeanne's Jar Chopped Salad

Caesar Salad with Grilled Chicken and Parmesan Crostini

Parmesan Crostini

Buttermilk Fried Chicken and Green Salad with Maple-Bacon Vinaigrette

Maple-Bacon Vinaigrette

Chicken and Orange Salad with Golden Beets

Oregon Summer Grilled Chicken Salad

Spicy Sriracha Buffalo Chicken Salad with Creamy Blue Cheese Dressing

Creamy Blue Cheese Dressing

Roasted Balsamic Chicken and Green Bean Salad with Goat Cheese

Thai Larb Chicken Salad

Thai Dressing

Chicken, Avocado, and Mango Salad

Chicken Salad Waldorf-Style

Simple Roast Chicken with Fingerling Potatoes

Lentil and Smoked Turkey Salad with Roasted Carrots and Parsnips on Peppery Greens

Mustard-Shallot Vinaigrette

Smoked Turkey and Red Greens Salad with Port Figs, Blue Cheese, and Whole-Wheat Croutons

Whole-Wheat Croutons

Smoked Duck Breast Salad with Haricots Verts, Apricots, and Pistachios

Duck Confit Salad with Fingerlings and Frisée

Sautéed Duck Breast Salad with Kumquats, Baby Broccoli, Dried Cherries, and Five-Spice Vinaigrette

OPPOSITE: Green Oak Leaf Lettuce

THE SUNDAY ROAST

The roast chicken dinner. Doesn't it evoke old-fashioned, home-and-hearth sentiments? A roast chicken, done right, is an across-the-board, hands-down winner. When it's paired with some potatoes, crisped in the chicken drippings, you have a dish worthy of the Sunday table. But did you know this time-tested favorite is part of a modern food movement?

This new way to cook is built around the concept of "repurposing." The idea is to help busy, time-pressed folks with their weekly menu planning by preparing a larger, more elaborate roast dinner on the weekend and then "repurposing" the leftovers into an easy, equally satisfying but spanking new dish for later in the week. Pork roast may beget tacos, pot roast could be fried into hash, and leftover roast chicken is shredded and transformed into a colorful, crunchy, fresh salad. Eating less of the "centerpiece" meat and more of the healthy surrounding vegetables is an intended added benefit.

Chicken is a natural in salad: the tender meat tastes great cold and gets nicely moistened and seasoned by dressing. It's a great source of lean protein and the texture and flavor enhance but do not overpower the other components. While some recipes in this book are crafted around a fresh or smoked cut of poultry, most feature pre-cooked chicken. For these salads you could use Roast Chicken Breasts (page 119), purchased rotisserie chicken, or chicken "repurposed." Because killing two birds with one stone is a good plan, I've included my Roast Chicken recipe at the end of this chapter (page 143). Being old-fashioned and modern all at once is a great way to cook, live, and eat.

CHINESE-STYLE CHICKEN SALAD
with Tangerines

Wolfgang Puck created a popular Chinese chicken salad for his Chinois restaurant in Santa Monica in the '80s. Since then, so many versions of this recipe have appeared on the scene. For my own version, I favor a mix with lots of colorful tangerines, green onions, and cilantro. The fried, puffy rice noodles called *mai fun* are strictly optional—I usually just add crunch to the salad by tossing in lots of toasted almonds and sesame seeds and don't bother with the deep-fried noodles. But if your heart is set on adding the dramatic-looking noodles, you can find them in the Asian section of most large supermarkets. Fried Wonton Strips (page 90) would also add that satisfying fried crunch if desired.

DRESSING

¼ cup rice wine vinegar

3 tablespoons soy sauce

2 tablespoons toasted peanut oil

2 tablespoons toasted sesame oil

1 generous tablespoon honey

2 teaspoons dry mustard

1 garlic clove, pressed

SALAD

6 cups (½-inch-thick crosswise slices) napa cabbage (about 1 small head)

6 cups mixed Asian greens, such as tatsoi and mizuna

5 small tangerines, peeled and separated into sections, or 3 oranges, peeled, halved, and thinly sliced

5 ounces sugar snap or snow peas, thinly sliced on diagonal (about 1 ⅓ cups)

¾ cup chopped celery

4 green onions, finely sliced

⅓ cup chopped fresh cilantro

Peanut oil for frying (optional)

1 ounce rice stick noodles (*mai fun*), broken into 2- to 3-inch pieces (optional)

12 ounces (about 3 cups) shredded cooked chicken breast (see recipe for Roast Chicken Breasts, page 119)

⅓ cup sliced almonds, toasted

2 tablespoons toasted sesame seeds, plus additional for sprinkling

Cilantro sprigs

FOR THE DRESSING: Whisk all ingredients to blend in a small bowl. *(Salad dressing can be prepared 2 days ahead; cover and refrigerate.)*

For the salad: Combine the cabbage, Asian greens, tangerines, peas, celery, green onions, and cilantro in a very large bowl. *(Salad can be prepared to this point up to 1 day ahead; cover and refrigerate.)*

If using the noodles: Heat 1 inch of peanut oil in a heavy medium skillet over high heat until almost smoking. Working in batches, add one-quarter of the noodles to the hot oil and fry until the noodles puff, about 10 seconds. Using tongs, carefully turn the noodles in the pan over if necessary to fry the noodles on the other side. Transfer the fried noodles to a pan to drain. Repeat with the remaining noodles.

Add the noodles (if using), chicken, almonds, and sesame seeds to the bowl with the salad. Whisk the dressing to blend and pour over the salad. Toss the salad to coat with the dressing. Divide the salad among 4 plates and sprinkle with additional sesame seeds. Garnish with cilantro sprigs and serve.

INDONESIAN SLAW
with Pineapple, Chicken, and Spicy Peanut Dressing

I was served a salad similar to this tasty slaw at the delightful Jungle Inn in Bukit Lawang, Sumatra, while visiting Gunung Leuser National Park and the orangutan rehabilitation center. The pineapple was such a refreshing addition to the shredded chicken, cabbage, and spicy peanut sauce. While my family and I were enjoying the salad (and several Bintang beers) by the rushing Bohorok River, we spotted a big mama orangutan and her attached baby in a very nearby tree. The cooks and servers at the inn had to come out with noisemakers to scare our beautiful red friend away—awesome! Along with lots of photos, I also came home with the inspiration for this recipe.

SPICY PEANUT DRESSING

1/3 cup (rounded) natural-style crunchy peanut butter

1/3 cup rice wine vinegar

2 tablespoons soy sauce

2 tablespoons (packed) golden brown sugar

1 tablespoon Sriracha sauce

1 large garlic clove, pressed

SLAW

8 cups thinly sliced cabbage (from about 1 medium head)

1/2 pineapple, peeled, cored, and cut into 1/2x2-inch strips

2 carrots, peeled and grated

1 red bell pepper, thinly sliced

4 green onions, thinly sliced

1/2 cup chopped fresh cilantro

1 pound shredded cooked chicken breast (see recipe for Roast Chicken Breasts, page 119)

1/2 cup chopped roasted and salted peanuts

FOR THE DRESSING: In a medium bowl, whisk together all ingredients to blend. Season the dressing to taste with salt.

For the slaw: In a large bowl, combine the cabbage, pineapple, carrots, red pepper, green onions, and cilantro. *(Salad can be made 8 hours ahead. Cover and refrigerate the cabbage mixture and dressing separately.)*

Add the shredded chicken and the dressing to the cabbage mixture and toss to combine. Season the slaw to taste with salt. Sprinkle with peanuts and serve.

CURRIED CHICKEN SALAD ON BABY SPINACH
with Mango Chutney Dressing and Garlic Naan Crisps

The full-flavored curried chicken salad is crunchy, savory, and sweet all at once—and it gets even better if it's made a day before serving. You can use leftover roast chicken, rotisserie chicken, or follow the recipe for Roast Chicken Breasts. Naan, Indian flatbread, is available at many specialty foods stores. If you can't find naan, go ahead and use pita bread to make the crisps.

CHICKEN SALAD

¼ cup Coffee Mug Mayo (page 183) or other mayonnaise

¼ cup sour cream

2 teaspoons curry powder

½ teaspoon kosher salt

12 ounces (about 3 cups) cooked chicken breast, diced (see recipe for Roast Chicken Breasts, page 119)

2 celery ribs, sliced

1 small pink lady or other crisp apple, peeled, cored, and diced

2 green onions, sliced

3 tablespoons currants or raisins

MANGO CHUTNEY DRESSING

¼ cup mango chutney

1 green onion, thinly sliced

2 tablespoons white balsamic vinegar

1 garlic clove, pressed

¼ cup almond or extra virgin olive oil

SPINACH SALAD AND GARNISH

10 cups baby spinach leaves or mixed greens

⅓ cup slivered almonds, toasted

¼ cup chopped fresh cilantro

Garlic Naan Crisps (page 119)

FOR THE CHICKEN salad: Whisk the mayonnaise, sour cream, curry powder, and salt to blend in a medium bowl. Add the chicken, celery, apple, green onions, and currants to the dressing in the bowl and stir to combine. Season the curry salad to taste with salt and pepper. *(Curry salad can be prepared up to 1 day ahead; cover and refrigerate.)*

For the spinach and dressing. In a small bowl, combine the chutney, green onion, vinegar, and garlic and stir to blend, mashing any large pieces in the chutney. Whisk in the oil and season to taste with salt and pepper.

In a separate large bowl, combine the spinach with enough dressing to season to taste and toss to coat. Divide the spinach among 4 plates.

Mix the almonds and cilantro into the curried chicken salad and mound in the center of the spinach on each plate, dividing evenly. Surround the salads with the Garlic Naan Crisps and serve.

Garlic Naan Crisps

Enjoy the crisps dipped into cucumber raita or an Indian mint-and-cilantro chutney.

3 tablespoons butter

1 garlic clove, pressed

1 tablespoon finely chopped fresh cilantro

2 pieces naan or pita breads

PREHEAT THE OVEN to 425°F. Melt the butter in a small saucepan over low heat; stir in the garlic and cilantro. Brush the breads evenly with the melted butter mixture. Cut the bread into 1½-inch-thick slices and arrange on a heavy large baking sheet. Bake until golden brown and crisp, about 8 minutes. Let cool completely. *(Chips can be made 1 day ahead. Cool and store in an airtight container or resealable plastic bag at room temperature.)*

Roast Chicken Breasts

| MAKES ABOUT 1 POUND OF COOKED CHICKEN

Basic roast chicken is simple to prepare and handy for fixing any number of main-course salads.

Extra virgin olive oil for brushing

2 large bone-in, skin-on chicken breast halves (about 1½ pounds)

Kosher salt

PREHEAT THE OVEN to 375°F. Brush olive oil on a shallow baking dish large enough to accommodate the chicken. Arrange the chicken in the prepared dish and sprinkle with kosher salt and pepper. Pour ¼ cup water into the baking dish. Cover the dish with a lid or aluminum foil and roast the chicken in the oven until no longer pink in the center or when an instant-read thermometer inserted into the thickest part of the chicken breast registers 180°F, about 40 minutes. Let the chicken cool completely. Remove and discard the skin and bones. Shred or dice the chicken according to the recipe, returning the chicken to the juices in the bottom of the pan. *(Chicken can be prepared up to 2 days ahead. Wrap the chicken in plastic and refrigerate.)*

RED MUSTARD AND BREAD SALAD
with Roast Chicken

This recipe pays tribute to Judy Rodgers and her restaurant, Zuni Café, in San Francisco. Rodgers, who got her start at Chez Panisse, wrote the excellent and inspiring *Zuni Café Cookbook*. In the book she details her technique for presalting meat and poultry, which guarantees moist and flavorful results. To taste Zuni Café's famous roast chicken is to truly appreciate her technique. The succulent chicken is cooked in a wood-fired oven, and the pan juices are tossed with a red mustard and bread salad. It's heavenly. This is my simplified *homage* to her remarkable dish.

6 chicken thighs (about 2½ pounds)

1 teaspoon kosher salt

4 cups (¾-inch) pieces rustic bread (from about ⅓ of a 1-pound loaf)

1 tablespoon extra virgin olive oil

2 garlic cloves, minced or pressed, divided

3 teaspoons chopped fresh thyme leaves, divided

8 cups red mustard leaves, torn into 4-inch pieces

½ cup chopped dried apricots

⅓ cup chopped toasted pistachios

1 green onion, finely sliced

1 cup chicken broth

RINSE THE CHICKEN and pat dry. Arrange the chicken thighs in a single layer in a shallow flameproof roasting pan. Sprinkle them on all sides with 1 generous teaspoon kosher salt. Cover loosely and refrigerate the chicken for at least 1 day and up to 2 days.

Preheat oven to 350°F. Place the bread pieces in a large bowl. Drizzle with the olive oil and sprinkle with 1 minced garlic clove and 1 teaspoon chopped fresh thyme. Sprinkle lightly with salt and toss well. Spread the bread pieces out on a heavy large rimmed baking sheet. Bake in the oven until lightly toasted, about 10 minutes. Return toasted bread pieces to same large bowl. *(Bread can be toasted up to 1 day ahead. Return to same large bowl and let cool. Cover and keep at room temperature.)*

Preheat oven to 475°F. Pat the chicken thighs dry and remove any moisture from the pan with a paper towel. Sprinkle chicken on all sides with remaining 2 teaspoons chopped fresh thyme and ground black pepper. Bake the chicken until browned and an instant-read thermometer inserted in the thickest part of the thigh registers 160° to 180°F, about 25 minutes.

Meanwhile, add the mustard greens, apricots, pistachios, and green onion to the bowl with the bread and toss to combine.

Transfer the chicken thighs to a cutting board. Add the chicken broth to the roasting pan. Stir the broth and the remaining minced garlic clove over medium-high heat, boiling

and stirring up the browned bits (deglazing), until the liquid is reduced to $^2/_3$ cup, about 2 minutes. Pour the hot pan reduction over the bread and greens in the bowl and toss to combine. If boneless chicken is desired, transfer the chicken to a cutting board and, using a large, sharp knife, cut the meat from the thighs along both sides of the bone. Arrange the chicken meat or thighs atop the greens and serve.

CHICKEN THIGHS

Shreds or chunks of tender, white breast meat are the standard for most chicken salads, but moist and succulent chicken thigh meat is an appetizing addition, too. Several of these recipes are prepared with thighs because they taste so great roasted and pan-fried. Because thighs are dark meat, they are more forgiving when cooked at high temperatures—they stay juicy inside while becoming browned with crisp bits on the outside. Another added bonus with chicken thighs: They're usually a lot less expensive than breast meat.

COBB SALAD

The cobb salad was invented in Hollywood at the Brown Derby Restaurant in the 1920s. It's such a fantastic salad and so up-to-date with bacon and blue cheese. Traditionally, the salad is served with a red-wine vinaigrette, but if you really want to go over the top, serve it with the Creamy Blue Cheese Dressing made with Roquefort (page 135).

8 ounces bacon, cut into ½-inch pieces

6 cups coarsely chopped romaine lettuce (from 1 head)

5 cups coarsely chopped watercress (from about 3 bunches)

2 cups coarsely chopped curly endive (from 1 small head)

12 ounces cooked boneless chicken breast, diced (about 3 cups; see recipe for Roast Chicken Breasts, page 119)

4 medium tomatoes, diced

2 ripe avocados, peeled, seeded, and diced

4 hardboiled eggs (page 97), chopped

4 ounces crumbled Roquefort cheese or other strong soft blue cheese

Mustard-Shallot Vinaigrette (page 145) or Creamy Blue Cheese Dressing (page 135)

FRY THE BACON in a heavy medium skillet over medium heat until crisp. Using a slotted spoon, transfer the bacon to paper towels or a brown paper bag to drain.

In a large bowl, combine the lettuce, watercress, and endive. To plate the salads individually: Divide the greens among 4 plates. Top the greens with the chicken, tomatoes, avocados, egg, cheese, and bacon, dividing evenly. Spoon desired dressing over the salads and serve. To toss the salad before serving: Add the chicken, tomatoes, avocados, egg, cheese, and bacon to the bowl with the greens. Toss the salad with enough dressing to season to taste and serve.

JEANNE'S JAR CHOPPED SALAD

Chef Suzanne Tracht created a crunchy cabbage salad for her acclaimed Los Angeles restaurant, Jar. It's a creative blend of ingredients, not beholden to any particular cuisine—just a thoughtful blend of color, flavor, and texture. The following recipe is not her "official" salad, but rather my own take on her ever-popular mix. Thinly sliced sourdough bread and sweet butter are perfect with this salad.

3 cups very thinly sliced green cabbage (about ¼ head)

2 cups very thinly sliced red cabbage, (about ¼ small head)

8 ounces (about 2 cups) shredded cooked chicken (see recipe for Roast Chicken Breast, page 119)

½ large fennel bulb, trimmed and very thinly sliced (about 2 cups)

¼ red onion, thinly sliced (about ½ cup)

¼ cup fresh Italian parsley leaves

6 brine-cured green olives, pitted and chopped (about 3 tablespoons)

Oregano Vinaigrette (page 52)

2½ ounces thinly sliced prosciutto, torn into pieces

2½ ounces feta cheese, crumbled (about ½ cup)

IN A LARGE bowl, combine both cabbages with the chicken, fennel, onion, parsley, and olives. Add enough Oregano Vinaigrette to coat, season the salad to taste with salt and freshly ground black pepper, and toss well. Divide the salad among 4 plates. Garnish with the prosciutto pieces, sprinkle with feta, and serve.

CAESAR SALAD
with Grilled Chicken and Parmesan Crostini

Purists who enjoy having a Caesar made tableside in a dark, red-booth restaurant with a cocktail in hand might scoff at this slightly nontraditional recipe for the famous Tijuana side salad—I omit the coddled egg from the dressing and top the greens with chicken. But it's just so good with grilled chicken as a main course— maybe that's why it's on just about every chain-restaurant menu. This homemade version is much better, and may even sway a traditionalist or two.

DRESSING

¹⁄₃ cup freshly squeezed lemon juice

1 tablespoon minced anchovy fillets (about 4 fillets)

2 garlic cloves, pressed

1 teaspoon Dijon mustard

1 teaspoon Worcestershire sauce

6 tablespoons extra virgin olive oil

¹⁄₂ teaspoon kosher salt

CHICKEN AND SALAD

1 pound boneless chicken breasts

5 cups arugula leaves

5 cups (from about 2 heads) romaine hearts, trimmed

2 green onions, thinly sliced

Parmesan Crostini (opposite)

¹⁄₂ cup Parmesan cheese shavings

FOR THE DRESSING: In a small bowl, whisk the lemon juice, anchovies, garlic, mustard, and Worcestershire sauce to blend. Gradually add the olive oil, whisking until emulsified. Whisk in the salt and season generously with cracked black pepper.

Arrange the chicken in a small baking dish. Add 2 tablespoons of the dressing and turn to coat. Marinate the chicken in the refrigerator for 2 to 6 hours.

Prepare a grill to medium heat or heat a grill pan over medium-high heat. Sprinkle the chicken with salt and pepper. Grill the chicken until browned and cooked through, about 6 minutes per side. Transfer the chicken to a cutting board and let stand 5 minutes.

Meanwhile, combine the arugula, romaine, and green onions in a large shallow bowl. Add about ¹⁄₄ cup dressing to season to taste and toss to coat. Divide the salad and Parmesan Crostini among 4 plates, arranging attractively. Slice the chicken breasts and arrange alongside the salad on each plate. Drizzle with some of the remaining dressing. Sprinkle salads with the Parmesan shavings, season with cracked black pepper, and serve.

Parmesan Crostini

12 thin slices ciabatta or rustic white bread
Extra virgin olive oil for brushing

¼ cup freshly grated Parmesan cheese

PREHEAT THE OVEN to 400°F. Arrange the bread pieces on a baking sheet and brush with olive oil. Sprinkle with the grated Parmesan and season with cracked black pepper. Bake until the crostini are golden brown and toasted, about 10 minutes. *(Crostini can be prepared 2 days ahead. Cool and store in an airtight container or resealable plastic bag.)*

BUTTERMILK FRIED CHICKEN AND GREEN SALAD with Maple-Bacon Vinaigrette

Who said salads were diet food? Hot-and-crunchy fried boneless chicken sits atop sweet and salty maple-bacon-flavored greens. Use a large cast-iron skillet to fry the bacon for the Maple-Bacon Vinaigrette, then add vegetable oil to the bacon drippings for frying the chicken so that you'll have only one pan to wash.

1¼ pounds boneless, skinless chicken breasts (about 2)

1 cup buttermilk

1 teaspoon hot pepper sauce (such as Tabasco)

1 teaspoon Worcestershire sauce

2 teaspoons kosher salt, divided

1 teaspoon ground black pepper, divided

½ teaspoon dried thyme, divided

1 cup all-purpose flour

1 teaspoon paprika

¼ teaspoon cayenne pepper

Vegetable oil for frying

14 cups mixed greens, such as green leaf and spinach

4 green onions, thinly sliced

Maple-Bacon Vinaigrette (opposite)

REMOVE THE TENDERLOIN from the chicken breasts. Place 1 chicken breast between sheets of plastic wrap. Using a mallet, pound the chicken until it is an even ½-inch thickness. Repeat with the remaining chicken breast. Stir the buttermilk, hot pepper sauce, Worcestershire sauce, 1 teaspoon kosher salt, ½ teaspoon pepper, and ¼ teaspoon thyme to blend in a shallow baking dish. Add the chicken breasts and the tenders. Turn the chicken to coat. Cover and marinate in the refrigerator for 1 to 6 hours.

Place a wire rack over a baking sheet. In another shallow baking dish that is large enough to accommodate a chicken breast, combine the flour, paprika, remaining 1 teaspoon salt, remaining ½ teaspoon pepper, cayenne, and remaining ¼ teaspoon thyme and stir to blend. Remove 1 chicken breast from the buttermilk mixture, allowing the excess to run off. Transfer the chicken to the flour mixture and turn to coat evenly with the flour mixture. Carefully place the chicken breast on the rack and repeat with the remaining chicken breast and tenders. Allow the chicken to stand 10 minutes. Carefully turn the chicken over and sprinkle any moist parts with the flour mixture.

Add enough vegetable oil to a very large heavy skillet to come 1 inch up the sides and heat over medium-high heat to 350°F. Carefully add the chicken to the oil. Fry until the chicken is golden brown and cooked through, turning once, about 10 minutes. Transfer the chicken to a paper towel to drain.

Toss the greens and the green onions in a bowl with 2/3 cup of the Maple-Bacon Vinaigrette. Divide the greens among 4 plates. Using a large knife or cleaver, cut each chicken breast crosswise into $\frac{1}{2}$-inch-thick slices. Arrange the chicken atop the salads, dividing evenly. Spoon the remaining dressing over the chicken and serve.

Maple-Bacon Vinaigrette

—— ┤ MAKES ABOUT 1 CUP

This would be awesome on a simple spinach salad.

6 thick slices applewood-smoked bacon (about 5 ounces)

3 tablespoons apple cider vinegar

3 tablespoons extra virgin olive oil

3 tablespoons pure maple syrup

1 generous teaspoon Dijon mustard

2 garlic cloves, pressed

FRY THE BACON in a heavy large skillet over medium heat, turning occasionally, until crisp. Using a slotted spoon, transfer the bacon to paper towels to drain. Let bacon cool to room temperature and finely chop.

In a medium bowl, whisk together the vinegar, oil, maple syrup, mustard, and garlic to blend. Stir in the chopped bacon. Season the dressing to taste with salt and pepper.

CHICKEN AND ORANGE SALAD with Golden Beets

Grated raw golden beets add crunch and flavor to this colorful blend. Rotisserie or leftover chicken can be used. Serve this with multigrain rolls or baguette slices.

2 large navel oranges

5 ounces golden beets (about 2 small), peeled and grated (about 1 cup packed)

2 tablespoons freshly squeezed lemon juice

3/4 teaspoon kosher salt, divided

3 tablespoons toasted walnut oil

1 small shallot, minced

1 tablespoon white balsamic vinegar

1 teaspoon honey

1/2 teaspoon finely grated orange peel

4 cups mixed baby greens, such as arugula, frisée, and baby romaine

1/2 large fennel bulb, trimmed and cut into very thin slices (about 1 cup)

8 ounces (about 2 cups) shredded cooked chicken (see recipe for Roast Chicken Breasts, page 119)

3 ounces crumbled goat cheese

1/3 cup toasted walnut pieces

CUT THE ORANGES into supremes (see note below). Squeeze the juice from the orange membranes into a medium bowl (about 2 tablespoons). Add the grated beets to the bowl and stir in 1 tablespoon lemon juice and 1/4 teaspoon salt and let stand at least 1 hour to soften the beets slightly.

In a small bowl, combine the oil, shallot, vinegar, honey, grated orange peel, remaining 1 tablespoon lemon juice, and remaining 1/2 teaspoon salt and whisk to blend. *(Salad can be prepared up to this point 1 day ahead. Cover the orange segments, beets, and dressing separately and refrigerate.)*

Combine the greens, fennel, and chicken in a large bowl. Top with the oranges and the beets with their juices. Scatter the cheese and walnuts over the salad. Pour over the dressing and sprinkle with fennel fronds. Toss the salad gently to combine and serve.

CITRUS SUPREMES

This French technique for preparing citrus is actually very easy. Many chefs recommend using a thin slicing knife, but I like to use a medium-size serrated knife. To start: Cut off the stem end of the fruit, just to the point of exposing the flesh. Cut off the opposite end. Place the fruit, cut-side down, on the work surface and cut away the peel and pith while following the contour of the flesh. Place the citrus on its side and cut carefully between the membranes to release the segments. This is an especially great way to serve grapefruit, as the membrane is so bitter. Pink grapefruit supremes topped with honey-flavored Greek yogurt make a heavenly breakfast or light dessert.

OREGON SUMMER GRILLED CHICKEN SALAD

4 SERVINGS

Inspired by a summer evening in the Pacific Northwest, this fruity salad makes use of local specialties such as peaches, hazelnuts, Oregon cheese, and pails of pails of roadside blackberries.

4 tablespoons white wine vinegar, divided

¼ cup plus 2 tablespoons hazelnut oil or extra virgin olive oil, divided

2 tablespoons honey, divided

1 teaspoon chopped fresh thyme or ¼ teaspoon dried thyme

1 teaspoon kosher salt, divided

1 pound (about 2 large) boneless chicken breasts, preferably with skin

2 tablespoons minced shallot

12 cups mixed greens

2 peaches, pitted and sliced

1 cup fresh blackberries

½ cup chopped toasted hazelnuts

2 ounces Oregon (or other) blue or soft, fresh goat cheese, crumbled

COMBINE 2 TABLESPOONS vinegar, 2 tablespoons oil, 1 tablespoon honey, the thyme, and ½ teaspoon salt in a small baking dish and stir to blend. Add the chicken and turn to coat. Cover and refrigerate 2 hours or up to overnight.

Preheat a grill or stovetop grill pan to medium heat. Grill the chicken until browned and cooked though, about 4 minutes per side. Transfer chicken to a cutting board.

In a large bowl, combine the remaining 2 tablespoons vinegar, remaining 1 tablespoon honey, and remaining ½ teaspoon salt. Gradually whisk in the remaining ¼ cup oil. Stir in the minced shallot. Add the greens, peaches, and blackberries to the dressing in the bowl and toss to combine. Divide the salad among 4 plates.

Thinly slice the warm chicken and arrange it atop the salads, dividing evenly. Drizzle any juices over the chicken. Sprinkle the salads with the hazelnuts and cheese and serve.

SPICY SRIRACHA BUFFALO CHICKEN SALAD
with Creamy Blue Cheese Dressing

Yes, this is a take on Buffalo wings—a Buffalo wing *salad* to be exact. And why not? There *is* something undeniably delicious about the combination of spicy-hot, vinegary chicken, the cooling crunch of celery sticks, and creamy blue cheese dressing. But while the bar and chain-restaurant versions of the popular happy-hour snack too often disappoint, this salad is a winner every time. Be sure to plan your craving ahead of time, as the chicken needs to marinate before cooking.

6 tablespoons apple cider vinegar

1/3 cup sriracha sauce

2 tablespoons paprika

1/2 teaspoon kosher salt

1 1/2 pounds boneless chicken thighs, cut into 1/2- to 3/4-inch strips

3 romaine hearts, cut crosswise into 1-inch-wide strips (about 12 cups)

4 celery ribs, thinly sliced

2 tablespoons butter

Creamy Blue Cheese Dressing (opposite)

1 cup sliced green onions

Additional blue cheese crumbles (about 2 ounces)

IN A LARGE bowl, combine the vinegar, sriracha, paprika, and salt and stir to blend. Add the chicken and stir to coat. Cover and refrigerate 8 hours or up to 2 days.

Combine the lettuce and the celery in a large bowl and set aside while cooking the chicken.

Melt the butter in a large, heavy, well-seasoned cast-iron or nonstick skillet over medium-high heat. Add the chicken and stir-fry until the chicken releases juices, about 4 minutes. Continue to cook the chicken until all the liquid in the pan evaporates and the chicken is coated and browned, about 3 minutes longer.

Toss the romaine and celery with enough of the Creamy Blue Cheese Dressing to coat and season to taste with salt and pepper. Divide the salad among 4 plates and top with the chicken. Sprinkle the salads with green onions and blue cheese crumbles and serve.

Creamy Blue Cheese Dressing

This is the classic—thick and rich with lots of blue cheese. Use it as a dip or spoon it over wedges of ice-cold lettuce.

2 ounces crumbled creamy blue cheese, such as Point Reyes, Maytag, or Roquefort

3 tablespoons finely chopped shallot

¼ cup sour cream

3 tablespoons extra virgin olive oil

1 tablespoon red wine vinegar

¼ teaspoon salt

1 to 3 tablespoons milk

WHISK THE BLUE cheese, shallot, sour cream, olive oil, vinegar, and salt to blend in a small bowl. Add enough milk to thin to a creamy yet pourable consistency. *(Dressing can be made up to 4 days ahead. Cover and refrigerate.)*

ROASTED BALSAMIC CHICKEN AND GREEN BEAN SALAD with Goat Cheese

Roasting at high temperature produces chicken that is succulent and green beans with intensified flavor. Roasting the chicken and the green beans in the same pan cuts down on dishes. This is a good salad for parties, as it's delicious served warm, at room temperature, or cold. Don't forget to pick up some really good rustic bread to serve with the salad and to marinate the chicken overnight.

CHICKEN

1/4 cup balsamic vinegar

2 tablespoons extra virgin olive oil

2 tablespoons chopped fresh thyme

6 garlic cloves, minced

1 1/2 pounds boneless, skinless chicken thighs

VINAIGRETTE

1/4 cup balsamic vinegar

3 tablespoons finely chopped shallot

1 tablespoon chopped fresh thyme leaves

2 garlic cloves, pressed

1/2 teaspoon kosher salt

1/2 cup extra virgin olive oil

SALAD

12 ounces green beans, trimmed

8 cups arugula

12 ounces cherry tomatoes, cut in half lengthwise

4 ounces goat cheese, crumbled

FOR THE CHICKEN: In a large bowl, combine the vinegar, oil, thyme, and garlic and whisk to blend. Add the chicken thighs and stir to blend. Cover and refrigerate the chicken overnight.

For the vinaigrette: Whisk the first 5 ingredients to blend in a small bowl. Gradually whisk in the olive oil. Season the dressing to taste with freshly ground black pepper. Set aside.

Preheat the oven to 450°F. Brush a heavy large rimmed baking sheet with olive oil. Pour the chicken with its marinade onto the prepared baking sheet and distribute evenly. Sprinkle with kosher salt and freshly ground black pepper. Roast the chicken in the oven until well browned and cooked through, about 30 minutes. Remove from the oven (maintain oven temperature). Using tongs, transfer the chicken to a cutting board. Add the green beans to the drippings on the roasting pan and stir well. Sprinkle the green beans with salt. Roast the green beans in the oven until just tender, about 8 minutes.

Cut the chicken into 2-inch pieces. Transfer the warm chicken and green beans to a large bowl. Add the arugula and tomatoes. Whisk the dressing to blend and pour it over the salad. Toss the salad. Sprinkle the salad with goat cheese and serve.

THAI LARB CHICKEN SALAD

Larb is a dumpy name for a sexy salad. Chopped chicken is sautéed with all sorts of aromatics and served atop a minty mix of cooling vegetables. Thai basil, lemon grass, and kaffir lime leaves can be found at Thai markets and some specialty foods stores. If you can't find the fresh lime leaves, double the amount of lemon grass. If neither lemon grass nor lime leaves are available, a scant teaspoon of grated lemon and lime peel will best approximate those flavors. Italian basil makes a fine substitute for the purple-tinged Thai variety.

$1\frac{1}{2}$ pounds boneless, skinless chicken thighs

$\frac{3}{4}$ cup coarsely chopped shallots

2 tablespoons thinly sliced lemon grass (about 1 stalk)

3 kaffir lime leaves, thinly sliced

1 small Thai green chile, stemmed, seeded, and sliced

1 teaspoon Thai fish sauce (*nam pla*)

1 red bell pepper, halved and thinly sliced

1 cup cucumber slices (from about 1 Persian or $\frac{1}{2}$ hothouse)

1 cup loosely packed mint leaves

2 green onions, thinly sliced

$\frac{1}{4}$ cup fresh basil leaves, preferably Thai basil, torn into small pieces

1 tablespoon peanut or vegetable oil

Lettuce leaves for lining plates, such as green leaf and Bibb

Thai Dressing (opposite)

COMBINE THE CHICKEN, shallots, lemon grass, lime leaves, chile, and fish sauce in the bowl of a food processor. Using on/off turns, pulse the mixture until $\frac{1}{4}$-inch pieces form. *(Can be prepared up to 1 day ahead. Cover and refrigerate.)*

In a medium bowl, combine the red pepper, cucumber, mint, green onions, and basil.

Heat the oil in a heavy large skillet over medium-high heat. Add the chicken mixture and fry, breaking the mixture into small pieces with a spatula, until cooked through and golden brown, about 12 minutes.

Meanwhile, line 4 plates with lettuce leaves. Top with the red pepper mixture, dividing evenly. Spoon the hot chicken mixture over the red pepper mixture, dividing evenly. Serve the salads, passing the Thai Dressing separately.

Thai Dressing

Fish sauce is a popular condiment in Southeast Asia. Although it is made with fermented anchovies and it smells rotten, it adds a layer of flavor to dishes that is both subtle and deliciously authentic. You can find fish sauce in the Asian section of some supermarkets, at Thai markets (where it is called *nam pla*) and at Vietnamese markets (where it is called *nuoc nam*). If there are no such markets in your area, it really is worth sourcing online.

¹/₃ cup freshly squeezed lime juice

3 tablespoons (packed) brown sugar

2 tablespoons fish sauce

2 teaspoons chili-garlic sauce or 1 teaspoon sambal oelek

COMBINE ALL THE ingredients in a small bowl and stir to blend. *(The dressing can be made 1 week ahead; cover and refrigerate.)*

CHICKEN, AVOCADO, AND MANGO SALAD

I like to toss all the ingredients for this salad in a big bowl so that the creamy avocados and the slippery mangoes luxuriously coat the rest of the ingredients. If you prefer, you can slice the avocado and mango and compose the ingredients on individual plates. You can use leftover roast chicken or a rotisserie bird in this simple yet colorful salad. Crisp, seeded flatbread crackers go well with the goodies here.

8 cups mixed greens, such as butter lettuce and/or green or red leaf lettuce

12 ounces (about 3 cups) shredded cooked chicken (see recipe for Roast Chicken Breasts, page 119)

2 firm-ripe mangoes, peeled, pitted, and cut into cubes

2 small firm-ripe avocados, peeled, pitted, and cut into cubes

1/4 red onion, thinly sliced

1/4 cup roasted and salted cashews

2 tablespoons minced fresh cilantro

Lime-Ancho Vinaigrette (page 39)

IN A LARGE bowl, combine the greens, chicken, mangoes, avocados, onion, cashews, and cilantro. Add enough Lime-Ancho Vinaigrette to season to taste (about 1/3 cup) and toss gently to combine.

CHICKEN SALAD WALDORF-STYLE

This is a delightfully old-fashioned salad. My grandmother served it along with a sandwich loaf that looked like a frosted layer cake at her ladies' luncheons. The original, created at the Waldorf Hotel in New York City in the 1890s, did not have chicken in it—and I'm sure it didn't have Belgian endive or Italian parsley in it either—but these additions perk up the flavor and color and give it a fresh update.

1½ tablespoons toasted walnut oil

2 teaspoons mayonnaise

1 teaspoon white wine vinegar

½ teaspoon Dijon mustard

¼ teaspoon kosher salt

6 ounces (about 1½ cups) shredded cooked chicken breast (see recipe for Roast Chicken Breasts, page 119)

1 medium red apple, cored and cut into julienne slices

2 celery ribs, cut into julienne slices

1 Belgian endive, cut into julienne slices

2 tablespoons currants

1 tablespoon minced fresh Italian parsley

Red leaf lettuce for lining plates (2 to 4 leaves; optional)

¼ cup walnuts, toasted and chopped

Parsley sprigs

IN A LARGE bowl, combine the first 5 ingredients and whisk to blend. Add the chicken, apple, celery, endive, currants, and parsley and toss well. Season the salad to taste with salt and pepper. Line 2 plates with red leaf lettuce, if desired. Divide the salad between plates. Sprinkle the salads with walnuts, garnish with the parsley sprigs, and serve.

BITE-SIZED PIECES

I have to admit that I'm partial to the French way of treating (and eating) salad greens. When the French serve salad, the leaves of lettuce are left whole, or at best with a large leaf of romaine, torn carefully in half. The French, so adept at eating with a knife *and* fork, gently fold the leaf of lettuce into a bite-sized bundle, pierce the bundle with the fork and voila, eat it. Here in the states, greens are often torn into small one- to two-inch pieces. Except when the salad is chopped, I like my greens on the larger side, and depending on the size of the leaf, I will keep it whole, or tear larger leaves into pieces about four inches wide.

SIMPLE ROAST CHICKEN with Fingerling Potatoes

This is great when accompanied by a big bowl of salad greens (yes, please!) tossed with Mustard-Shallot Vinaigrette (page 145). If you are like me, then you would make a bed of those fabulous greens for your chicken and potatoes and . . . turn this into one more "salad for dinner." And leftover chicken from this recipe can be used to make almost any of the chicken salads in this chapter.

1 pound fingerling or new potatoes, cut in half lengthwise

3 tablespoons extra virgin olive oil, divided

2 tablespoons chopped fresh thyme leaves, divided

2 garlic cloves, pressed

1 (3- to 4-pound) fryer chicken

1 teaspoon kosher salt

1/2 cup dry white wine

1/4 cup chicken broth

TOSS THE POTATOES with 2 tablespoons olive oil and 1 tablespoon thyme leaves in a 15x11-inch roasting pan or baking dish until well coated. In a small bowl, mix together the remaining 1 tablespoon olive oil, 1 tablespoon thyme leaves, and the garlic. Nestle the chicken in the roasting pan in the center of the potatoes. Rub the garlic oil mixture over the entire surface of the chicken. Sprinkle the kosher salt over the potatoes and chicken. Grind some black pepper over all. *(Chicken can be prepared up to this point 4 hours ahead. Cover with waxed paper and refrigerate.)*

Preheat the oven to 400°F. Place the chicken and potatoes in the oven and roast 15 minutes. Reduce the temperature to 375°F and continue roasting, stirring the potatoes once or twice, until an instant-read thermometer inserted into the chicken thigh registers 160°F. Transfer the chicken to a platter along with the potatoes.

Add the wine and broth to the roasting pan and stir to scrape up the browned bits on the bottom of the pan. Place the pan in the oven for 5 minutes. Season the pan juices to taste with salt and pepper and transfer to a small pitcher or bowl. Cut the chicken into serving pieces and serve, passing the pan juices separately.

LENTIL AND SMOKED TURKEY SALAD
with Roasted Carrots and Parsnips on Peppery Greens

Vacuum-sealed steamed lentils, available at most specialty foods stores, are a flavorful convenience if you want to save time cooking the lentils. In the summer, you can transform this simple, hearty salad into a no-cook affair by replacing the roasted parsnips and carrots with $1^{1}/_{2}$ cups halved cherry tomatoes and a diced cucumber.

$1^{1}/_{2}$ cups French green (du Puy) lentils

$^{1}/_{2}$ teaspoon kosher salt

12 ounces carrots (about 3), peeled and cut into $^{1}/_{3}$-inch-thick slices

12 ounces parsnips (about 2 large), peeled, quartered, and cut into $^{1}/_{3}$-inch-thick slices

2 tablespoons extra virgin olive oil, plus additional for brushing

8 ounces smoked turkey, cut into $^{1}/_{2}$-inch cubes

1 tablespoon chopped fresh thyme leaves

$^{1}/_{4}$ cup (or more) Mustard-Shallot Vinaigrette (opposite)

10 cups peppery greens, such as arugula, red mustard, mizuna, and spinach

BRING 5 CUPS water, lentils, and kosher salt to a boil in a heavy medium saucepan. Simmer over medium heat until the lentils are tender and the liquid is absorbed, about 35 minutes. Remove from the heat and let cool to room temperature.

Meanwhile, preheat the oven to 450°F. Brush a heavy large baking sheet with olive oil. In a large bowl, toss the carrots and parsnips with the 2 tablespoons olive oil. Spread the vegetables out in a single layer on the prepared baking sheet and sprinkle with salt. Roast the carrots and parsnips in the oven until tender and browned, turning once, about 15 minutes.

In the same large bowl used for the carrots and parsnips (do not wash), combine the cooked lentils, turkey, thyme, and 2 tablespoons of the Mustard-Shallot Vinaigrette and toss to combine.

Stir the roasted carrots and parsnips into the lentil mixture. Toss the greens in another large bowl with 2 tablespoons vinaigrette to coat. Divide the greens among 4 plates. Top with the lentil mixture, dividing evenly, and serve.

Mustard-Shallot Vinaigrette

This is a classic French vinaigrette that's wonderful on practically all green salads.

3 tablespoons red wine vinegar

1 rounded tablespoon minced fresh shallot

2 teaspoons Dijon mustard

½ teaspoon kosher salt

⅓ cup extra virgin olive oil

WHISK THE FIRST 4 ingredients to blend in a small bowl; gradually whisk in the oil until emulsified. *(The vinaigrette can be made 1 week ahead. Cover and refrigerate. Bring the vinaigrette to room temperature and whisk to blend before using.)*

DRESS IT UP

Salad dressing is not only good to eat, it's good for the mind. A recent study conducted by Columbia University confirms that eating salad without dressing is both not tasty and not beneficial to the cerebrum. More specifically, research shows that homemade olive oil-and-vinegar salad dressings eaten in conjunction with a diet rich in nuts, fish, tomatoes, poultry, fruits, cruciferous and dark and leafy green vegetables lessen the risk of developing Alzheimer's disease. Hmm, sounds like the makings of a good salad

SMOKED TURKEY AND RED GREENS SALAD
with Port Figs, Blue Cheese, and Whole-Wheat Croutons

Plumping dried Mission figs in ruby port intensifies their flavor and makes a compelling combo with the blue cheese and smoky turkey.

16 dried Mission figs, cut in half

1 cup ruby port

12 cups mixed red greens, such as red oakleaf, red romaine, and radicchio

8 ounces smoked turkey, cut into 1/2 x 3-inch slices

Mustard-Shallot Vinaigrette (page 145)

3 ounces blue cheese, crumbled

Whole-Wheat Croutons, (below)

1 teaspoon fresh thyme leaves

COMBINE THE FIGS and port in a heavy small saucepan. Simmer over low heat until the port is absorbed and the figs are tender, about 12 minutes. Remove from the heat and let cool. *(Figs can be prepared up to 1 week ahead. Transfer to a jar, seal, and refrigerate.)*

In a large bowl, combine the greens, turkey, and 2 tablespoons Mustard-Shallot Vinaigrette and toss to coat. Divide the salad among 4 plates. Garnish each salad with figs, cheese, croutons, and thyme leaves, dividing evenly. Season the salads with cracked black pepper and serve, passing the remaining vinaigrette separately.

Whole-Wheat Croutons

MAKES ABOUT 4 CUPS

These are a crunchy and wholesome addition to robust greens. Be sure to use a sugar-free whole-wheat or whole-grain bread for the best taste.

1/4 cup extra virgin olive oil

2 garlic cloves, pressed

6 ounces (about 4 slices) whole-wheat bread, such as pain au levain or sprouted 7-grain bread, cut into 1/2- to 3/4-inch cubes (about 4 cups)

PREHEAT THE OVEN to 400°F. In a medium bowl, combine the olive oil and garlic. Add the bread cubes and toss to coat. Spread the cubes out on a heavy large baking sheet. Season with salt and bake until lightly toasted, about 10 minutes. *(Croutons can be prepared 1 day ahead. Let cool completely and store in an airtight container.)*

146   SALAD FOR DINNER

SMOKED DUCK BREAST SALAD
with Haricots Verts, Apricots, and Pistachios

Smoked duck breast makes this salad fancy enough for summer entertaining. You can find the smoked duck breast at specialty foods stores, or online from D'Artagnan (dartagnan.com). Pick up the pistachio oil at fancy food shop or substitute extra virgin olive oil. If peaches are more abundant than apricots, go ahead and use four medium-sized peaches instead. In the fall, Fuyu persimmons are perfect in place of the apricots.

12 ounces haricots verts (thin green beans), trimmed, or regular green beans, trimmed and cut on a diagonal into 2-inch lengths

1/3 cup pistachio oil or extra virgin olive oil

3 tablespoons white balsamic vinegar

1/2 teaspoon kosher salt

6 cups mixed baby greens

8 apricots, pitted and quartered

1/4 cup chopped red onion

8 to 12 ounces smoked duck breast, thinly sliced

1/3 cup chopped roasted shelled pistachios

COOK THE BEANS in a pot of rapidly boiling salted water until crisp-tender, about 3 minutes. Transfer them to a bowl of ice water to cool rapidly. Drain and pat dry with a clean dish towel. *(Haricots verts can be cooked 1 day ahead. Cover with plastic and refrigerate.)*

Whisk the oil, vinegar, and salt to blend in a small bowl for the dressing.

Divide the greens and haricots verts among 4 plates. Divide the apricots among the plates and sprinkle with the onion. Arrange the duck slices atop the salads, dividing evenly. Drizzle the salads with the dressing and season with cracked black pepper. Sprinkle the salads with the pistachios and serve.

DUCK CONFIT SALAD with Fingerlings and Frisée

| 2 SERVINGS

Duck confit hails from the southwest of France; it is duck that has been salt-cured and then slowly cooked in fat. You can find it sold in cans and vacuum-sealed plastic packages at French import stores or online from U.S. or Canadian sources, such as D'Artagnan (dartagnan.com). The tart vinegar and the slightly bitter greens cut the sweet, fat richness of the duck and crispy potatoes. Serve this hearty salad on a fall or winter evening with a nice glass of French or early-season California or Oregon Pinot Noir.

2 tablespoons finely chopped shallot

4 teaspoons best-quality red wine vinegar, preferably Banyuls vinegar

1 tablespoon extra virgin olive oil

¼ teaspoon kosher salt

2 tablespoons duck fat or olive oil

12 ounces small fingerling potatoes or other baby potatoes (about 14), cut in half lengthwise

1 duck leg confit, boned and shredded into bite-sized pieces of meat (about 1⅓ to 1½ cups)

6 cups frisée, separated into leaves, larger leaves torn in half

1 Belgian endive, cut into 1-inch pieces

PREHEAT THE OVEN to 250°F.

In a large bowl, combine the shallot, vinegar, olive oil, and salt and whisk to blend; set the vinaigrette aside.

Heat the fat in a heavy large skillet over medium heat. Add the potatoes, cut side down, and fry undisturbed until evenly golden brown on the bottom, about 8 minutes. Turn the potatoes and fry until tender and crisp, about 7 minutes. Transfer the potatoes to a small roasting pan and sprinkle with salt. Keep the potatoes warm in the oven.

Add the duck to the same skillet (no need to wash the skillet) and stir-fry over medium-high heat until golden brown in parts and heated through, about 4 minutes.

Meanwhile, add the frisée and the endive to the bowl with the vinaigrette and toss well. Arrange the frisée mixture on 2 plates and top with the duck, dividing evenly. Surround the salads with the potatoes. Season the salads with freshly ground black pepper and serve.

The Mother of All Vinegars

I HAVE THE GOOD FORTUNE TO HAVE AN ENDLESS SUPPLY OF FINE 2-YEAR, oak-aged, house-made red wine vinegar. I don't ferment it myself, but I like to think that I can take a little credit for it. On a visit to France a number of years ago, I was struck by the clean, complex flavor of the vinaigrettes dousing the salads at the end of meals. Those dressings, it turns out, were made with homemade wine vinegar. Vinegar is alcohol that has been fermented into acetic acid. The fermentation occurs when a "mother," a mix of cellulose and acetic acid bacteria, reacts with oxygen in the air. You'll find vinegar mother in better-quality commercial vinegars—it's that weird, slimy stuff at the bottom of the bottle.

Because I expressed interest in making my own vinegar, a jar of a dark and slimy liverlike substance was thrust my way by one of my generous and exuberant French friends. I fretted just a little about bringing the weird jar of bizarre content through customs, but once in line, I forgot all about my "mother"—so much so, that I left the satchel on the carpet behind me while meandering through the long line to the officials. It wasn't until the following day that I noticed that the important bag was missing. Luckily, airport employees found the case and connected it to my flight. It was delivered to the ticketing counter for safe keeping, and I was able to scoop up the satchel the following day, contents intact, without having to explain to the customs official just what that ghastly looking thing was.

Alas, my foray into the vinegar arts did not go so well. Maybe my kitchen is too sunny and often hot, maybe my husband and I have the habit of *finishing* the nightly bottle of wine and I didn't feed the mother enough. My brew burned the eyes and nostrils and was better suited to removing paint than making vinaigrette. Good thing I'd had the foresight to split the mother with one of my brothers (the brother who happens to make wine). In his cool cellar, combined with a better quality and quantity of wine, not to mention some oak aging, the mother produced a mighty fine blend—a vinegar that weds beautifully with olive oil and adds depth to my salads and brings about fond thoughts of friends, family, and France.

SAUTÉED DUCK BREAST SALAD with Kumquats, Baby Broccoli, Dried Cherries, and Five-Spice Vinaigrette

The technique of slowly rendering the fat from the duck skin prior to cooking the meat results in crispy, completely edible, and delicious skin. If you start the duck in a cold skillet, it will stick to the pan as the fat melts, allowing you to easily pour off the melted fat while cooking. Kumquats add a sweet-tart and aromatic touch to this elegant salad. Currant dinner rolls from a good bakery round out the meal.

FIVE-SPICE VINAIGRETTE

2 tablespoons minced shallot

1 tablespoon balsamic vinegar

1 garlic clove, pressed

1 teaspoon toasted sesame oil

1/2 teaspoon kosher salt

1/2 teaspoon five-spice powder

3 tablespoons extra virgin olive oil

SALAD

4 small or 2 large duck breasts (about 1 pound)

1 bunch baby broccoli, trimmed and cut into 1 1/2-inch pieces

7 cups arugula

5 kumquats, cut into thin rounds

1/3 cup dried sour cherries or dried cranberries

1/4 cup toasted sliced almonds

FOR THE VINAIGRETTE: In a small bowl, combine the first 6 ingredients and whisk to blend. Gradually whisk in the olive oil.

For the salad: Arrange the duck breasts, skin side down, in a cold heavy large skillet. Set the skillet over medium-low heat and cook the duck until most of the fat is rendered from the skin and the meat is not cooked, pouring off the fat occasionally (reserve the fat for another use), about 20 minutes. Using a spatula, loosen the duck from the bottom of the skillet and increase the heat to medium-high. Cook the duck until the skin is well browned and crisp, about 3 minutes. Turn the duck and cook until just browned on the meat side, about 2 minutes for medium-rare. Transfer the duck to a cutting board and let stand 5 minutes.

Meanwhile, fill a medium skillet with 1 inch of water. Generously salt the water and bring to a boil. Add the baby broccoli and cover and cook until the broccoli is crisp-tender, about 2 minutes. Drain the broccoli and plunge into bowl of ice water to cool. Drain well.

In a large bowl, combine the arugula, baby broccoli, kumquats, cherries, and almonds. Add 3 tablespoons of the vinaigrette and toss well. Divide the salad among 4 plates. Thinly slice the duck. Arrange the duck slices atop the salads, dividing evenly. Drizzle the remaining dressing over the duck slices. Drizzle any duck juices from the cutting board over the salads and serve.

SALADS with Meat

Frisée and Arugula Salad with Bacon, Poached Egg, and Whole-Wheat Croutons

Kale and Cornbread Salad

Buttermilk Cornbread

Baby Greens with Quince Vinaigrette and Artisanal Cheeses and Charcuterie

Quince Vinaigrette

Spanish Chopped Salad with Migas

Summertime Corn and Ham Salad

Bresaola and Arugula Salad with Parmesan Shavings and Lemon-Chive Drizzle

Mixed Greens with Farro, Bacon, Dates, Walnuts, Pears, and Parmesan

Italian Chopped Salad

Fig, Fennel, and Barley Salad with Bucheron, Speck, and Honey-Spice Walnuts

Honey-Spice Glazed Walnuts

Croque Madame dans le Jardin

Steakhouse Salad

Argentine Grilled Steak and Vegetable Salad with Chimichurri Vinaigrette

Korean Barbecue Beef Salad

Caribbean Salad with Jerk Pork

Roast Beef with Red Leaf Lettuce, Red Onions, Radishes, and Horseradish Cream

Thai-Style Grilled Beef Salad

Vietnamese Pork Meatball Banh Mi Salad

Coffee-mug Mayo

Grilled Pork and Green Onions with Romesco Sauce, Greens, and Sherry Vinaigrette

Romesco Sauce

Oakleaf Lettuce with Grilled Pork, Corn, and Nectarines with Honey-Marjoram Vinaigrette

Honey-Marjoram Vinaigrette

Trio of Grated Salads with Hearty Greens and Pan-Seared Sausages

Lamb Rib Chops with Cracked Wheat, Mint, and Asian Apple Pear Salad

Fattoush Salad with Lamb

Mediterranean Lemon Dressing

Grilled Lamb Kebabs

Grilled Kale with Lamb and Garlic-Mint Yogurt Dressing

THE MIGHTY GREEN

When my girls were little, we used to play a silly game: name a food that doesn't taste good with peanut butter. This isn't so easy because peanut butter, in an abstract way (think Thai or West African peanut sauce) combines delectably with most flavors, sweet or savory. (Of course to play the game, you have to like peanut butter.) To a certain extent, this game can be played with my favorite salad green, arugula. What savory dish isn't improved by a few fresh sprigs of artfully arranged arugula?

I am a huge fan of arugula—aka rocket, roguette, rugula, and rucola. This member of the mustard family is native to the Mediterranean, grows wildly in Asia, and is cultivated wordwide—notably, in my backyard. Indeed, I have become a rocket connoisseur, planting different varieties and discovering favorites such as Runway with pretty oak-shaped leaves. We plant seeds successively to pluck fresh bunches year-round. Many advise picking the leaves young and mild, but I love them mature, bold, and hot. I use it as a garnish on my morning egg, for lunch in a salad or on a sandwich, and for dinner as a big component, especially when I serve meat.

A bouquet of arugula is the perfect foil to meat—it provides a punch of bright green flavor and toothsome textural contrast. Because it stands up well to heat, arugula complements roasts, steaks, and braises, especially when the leaves are lightly coated in sauce, au jus, or gravy. It's funny to me that this plant was once considered so chichi, because now, at least in my kitchen, it's as common as, say, peanut butter.

FRISÉE AND ARUGULA SALAD
with Bacon, Poached Egg, and Whole-Wheat Croutons

Salade Lyonnaise is a French bistro classic made with frisée lettuce, lardons, and a poached egg. I like this salad with a hefty portion of greens that includes arugula. Sprinkled with lots of crunchy croutons, this is heavenly eaten from a deep bowl for breakfast, lunch, or dinner. If you prefer, you can simply fry the eggs in the skillet of bacon drippings instead of poaching them.

4 slices applewood-smoked bacon, cut into ½-inch pieces

1 tablespoon white wine vinegar

2 eggs

4 cups frisée lettuce, torn into bite-sized pieces

3 cups arugula leaves, torn into pieces

Mustard-Shallot Vinaigrette (page 145)

2 cups Whole-Wheat Croutons (page 146)

FRY THE BACON in a heavy medium skillet over medium heat until crisp. Using a slotted spoon, transfer the bacon to paper towels or a brown paper bag to drain.

Bring a medium skillet of water to a gentle simmer over medium heat. Add the vinegar to the water. Working with one egg at a time, crack an egg into a small bowl and gently slide the egg into the simmering water in the skillet. Poach the eggs, gently pushing simmering water over the tops until the whites are cooked through but the yolks are not set, about 3 minutes.

Meanwhile, toss the greens in a large bowl with enough Mustard-Shallot Vinaigrette to season the salad (about 2 tablespoons). Divide the salad between 2 plates or bowls. Using a slotted spoon, drain the eggs carefully and place 1 atop each salad. Season the egg and salad with cracked black pepper. Sprinkle the bacon and the croutons over the salads, dividing evenly, and serve.

KALE AND CORNBREAD SALAD

When my editor asked if I was going to make a cornbread salad for this book, I replied, "Sure. Is that like a Southern take on a panzanella?" The salad I began to conjure in my head was radically different from the traditional cornbread salad that many Southerners grew up with. The authentic version resembles a trifle with layers of cubed cornbread, cubed ham, diced tomatoes, grated cheese, chopped onions, pinto beans (yep, pinto beans), lots of sour cream and ranch dressing, and maybe a little lettuce. It could be good, but not quite what I had imagined—a blend of dark greens, ham, a touch of sharp cheddar, cornbread, all dressed with a light buttermilk dressing. The fruition of this salad is something that should not only please you, but also my Southern editor.

1/3 cup buttermilk

2 tablespoons extra virgin olive oil

1 tablespoon freshly squeezed lemon juice

1 tablespoon white wine vinegar

1 garlic clove, pressed

1/2 teaspoon kosher salt

1 bunch kale, center ribs removed, leaves cut crosswise into 1-inch-thick pieces (about 6 cups)

3 ounces best-quality ham, such as applewood-smoked or cured Black Forest ham

1/3 cup grated extra-sharp white cheddar

2 cups (3/4-inch) cubes of Buttermilk Cornbread (page 159) lightly toasted (about 4 ounces)

IN A LARGE bowl, combine the buttermilk, olive oil, lemon juice, vinegar, garlic, and salt and whisk to blend. Add the kale and toss to combine well. Let the kale salad marinate until the leaves become tender, stirring occasionally, about 30 minutes. *(The salad can be prepared up to this point about 2 hours ahead. Cover and refrigerate.)*

Mix the ham and cheese into the kale salad. Very gently fold the cornbread into the salad. Season with cracked black pepper and serve.

Buttermilk Cornbread

MAKE ONE 9X9-INCH LOAF

This is a good all-purpose loaf of cornbread that is heavenly when served warm with butter and honey. Leftovers are great in the cornbread salad. Best-quality cornmeal results in better cornbread.

1/4 cup (1/2 stick) unsalted butter

1 1/4 cups stone-ground cornmeal

3/4 cup unbleached all-purpose flour

1 tablespoon sugar

1 1/2 teaspoons baking powder

1 teaspoon kosher salt

1/2 teaspoon baking soda

1 1/4 cups buttermilk

1 large egg

PREHEAT THE OVEN to 350°F. Melt the butter in a 9x9-inch baking pan in the oven. In a medium bowl, combine the cornmeal, flour, sugar, baking powder, salt, and baking soda and whisk to blend. Whisk in the buttermilk, then the egg. Pour all but 1 tablespoon butter from the hot baking pan into the batter and whisk to combine. Pour the batter into the hot pan, spreading to even. Bake until a tester inserted into the center comes out clean, about 20 minutes. *(Cornbread can be prepared 1 day ahead. Cover tightly with foil.)*

BABY GREENS with Quince Vinaigrette, Artisanal Cheeses, and Charcuterie

This salad showcases your favorite cheeses and cured meats. I like to use Humboldt Fog, a soft-ripened goat cheese made by Cypress Grove Chèvre; Point Reyes Blue; and Roth Käse cheeses with La Quercia prosciutto and Fra' Mani salumi piccante. You can serve any cheeses with this salad, but a good rule of thumb (as with a cheese course) is to feature one goat cheese, one blue cheese, and one firm, aged cheese. If you have a good cheese store in your neighborhood, ask the cheesemonger for some good, preferably local, suggestions. Quince paste, sometimes labeled *membrillo*, is available at cheese shops, online, and at specialty foods stores.

8 cups mixed baby greens

Quince Vinaigrette (opposite)

4 slices soft-ripened goat cheese, such as Humboldt Fog, or other goat cheese

4 small wedges aged blue cheese

4 slices firm, aged cow's or sheep's milk cheese, such as aged Gouda, Manchego, or Petit Basque

16 slices artisanal salami or Spanish dry-cured chorizo

12 slices prosciutto

½ cup toasted almonds

1 small tart apple, cored and thinly sliced

French bread baguette slices

IN A LARGE bowl, toss the greens with enough Quince Vinaigrette to coat lightly. Divide the greens among 4 large plates. Season the salads with cracked black pepper. Arrange the cheeses, meats, almonds, and apple slices around the greens, dividing evenly, and serve with baguette slices.

A COMPOSED SALAD

Is your salad calm, cool, and collected? Generally, salads are chopped (think Cobb), tossed (think Caesar), or composed. A composed salad is simply a salad where the ingredients are artfully arranged on a plate or in a shallow bowl. Because these salads are so lovely to behold, dressing is served separately or spooned with a flourish over the components. Composed salad comes from the French *salade composée,* and here the "composed" is a verb, not an adjective describing the salad's mood.

Quince Vinaigrette

This mild, sweet dressing is great on any salad or sandwich that includes cheese.

¼ cup white wine vinegar

3 tablespoons quince paste (*membrillo*)

1 garlic clove, peeled

½ teaspoon kosher salt

½ cup extra virgin olive oil

COMBINE THE VINEGAR, quince paste, garlic clove, and salt in a blender. Blend until the quince paste is smooth. Add the olive oil and pulse briefly until blended. Season the dressing to taste with freshly ground black pepper. *(Dressing can be made 1 week ahead. Cover and refrigerate. Bring the dressing to room temperature and whisk to blend before using.)*

SPANISH CHOPPED SALAD with Migas

Migas, a Spanish version of croutons, are bits of firm-textured bread sautéed in olive oil until golden and crisp. Along with some Marcona almonds, they add crunch to this array of Spanish delicacies.

MIGAS

¼ cup extra virgin olive oil

3 cups coarse fresh breadcrumbs (¼- to ½-inch pieces)

2 garlic cloves, minced

SALAD

4 cups coarsely chopped arugula

4 cups coarsely chopped romaine

1 tart green apple, cored and diced

1 red bell pepper, diced

½ cup chopped sweet onion

4 ounces diced Manchego cheese (about 1 cup)

3 ounces diced peeled dry-cured Spanish chorizo (about ⅔ cup)

6 to 8 tablespoons Quince Vinaigrette (page 161)

⅔ cup chopped Marcona or other roasted almonds

FOR THE MIGAS: Heat the olive oil in a heavy large skillet over medium heat. Add the bread and stir with a wooden spoon to coat with olive oil. Stir in the garlic and sprinkle with salt and pepper. Sauté the migas until golden brown and chewy-crisp, about 8 minutes. Remove the skillet from the heat and cool completely. *(The migas can be made 1 day ahead. Store at room temperature in an airtight container.)*

For the salad: In a large bowl, combine the arugula, romaine, apple, red pepper, onion, Manchego, and chorizo. Add enough Quince Vinaigrette to season the salad to taste and toss to coat. Mix half of the almonds and migas into the salad. Sprinkle the salad with the remaining almonds and migas and serve.

SUMMERTIME CORN AND HAM SALAD

I make this salad in the summer with random ingredients plucked from the garden mixed with farmers' market corn. You can easily adapt this no-cook salad depending on what's in your garden or grocery basket. It's perfect for a picnic.

⅓ cup extra virgin olive oil

3 tablespoons red wine vinegar

2 garlic cloves, pressed or minced

½ teaspoon kosher salt

4 ears fresh corn

8 ounces ham, diced

2 tomatoes, diced, or 1 pint cherry tomatoes, quartered

1 medium zucchini, diced

1 small cucumber, diced

1 Fresno or jalapeño pepper, seeded and finely diced

2 tablespoons chopped fresh herbs, such as basil, thyme, and oregano

3 cups mâche or baby arugula

WHISK THE FIRST 4 ingredients to blend in a large bowl. Holding an ear of corn perpendicular to a cutting board and using a large sharp knife, cut the kernels from the cob. Repeat with remaining ears of corn. Add the kernels to the oil and vinegar mixture in the large bowl. Add the ham, tomatoes, zucchini, cucumber, pepper, and herbs and mix well. Season the salad to taste with salt and pepper. (The salad can be prepared up to this point 6 hours ahead. Cover and refrigerate.)

Stir the mâche into the salad and serve immediately.

BRESAOLA AND ARUGULA SALAD
with Parmesan Shavings and Lemon-Chive Drizzle

Bresaola, sometimes called beef prosciutto, is dried and cured beef—it's delicious with the tart greens and nutty Parmesan shavings. The addition of orzo to this classic Italian antipasto makes for an excellent light supper, especially when paired with a food-friendly red Italian wine such as a Montepulciano. Start the meal with ripe melon slices and end with gelato and cookies. If you can't find the bresaola, use prosciutto.

$3/4$ cup orzo pasta	$1/4$ teaspoon grated lemon zest
4 tablespoons extra virgin olive oil, divided	$1/8$ teaspoon kosher salt
1 garlic clove, pressed	6 ounces thinly sliced bresaola
3 tablespoons snipped chives	4 cups arugula
2 tablespoons freshly squeezed lemon juice	2 ounces Parmesan cheese shavings

COOK THE ORZO in a small pot of generously salted rapidly boiling water until tender yet firm to the bite. Drain the orzo (do not rinse) and transfer it to a large bowl. Stir in 1 tablespoon of the olive oil and the garlic and let cool completely.

In a small bowl, combine the remaining 3 tablespoons olive oil, the chives, lemon juice, lemon zest, and salt and whisk to blend. Season the lemon-chive drizzle with freshly ground black pepper.

Arrange the bresaola slices in a single layer on a platter or on each of 4 plates, dividing evenly. Add the arugula to the orzo and add enough lemon-chive drizzle to coat lightly. Spoon the arugula mixture atop the bresaola and sprinkle with the Parmesan shavings. Spoon remaining drizzle around the bresaola and serve.

PARMESAN SHAVINGS

Parmesan shavings are easy to make. Start with a wide chunk of Parmesan cheese and, using a vegetable peeler (a sharp one helps here), shave off paper-thin slices of cheese. So that you don't break the delicate shavings when transferring them to the salad bowl, make the shavings over a piece of waxed paper for easy transport or simply shave the cheese directly over the salad.

MIXED GREENS
with Farro, Bacon, Dates, Walnuts, Pears, and Parmesan

Nutty, chewy, salty, sweet, and juicy—this salad has it all. Toasting the walnuts and the farro in the bacon drippings adds extra depth of flavor to the salad. Deglet Noor is a variety of date that is often available pitted. The firm-textured date slices into neat, cute rounds, but you can also use a softer date, such as a Medjool. Simply pit the dates and shred them into thin strips with your fingertips.

½ cup farro (semipearled or pearled wheat berries)

6 ounces best-quality bacon

½ cup walnuts

¼ cup toasted walnut oil or extra virgin olive oil

2 tablespoons balsamic vinegar

2 garlic cloves, pressed

¼ teaspoon kosher salt

6 cups mixed greens

1 pear, halved, cored, and thinly sliced

½ red onion, very thinly sliced

12 pitted Deglet Noor dates, cut into rounds

3 ounces thin shavings Parmesan cheese

BOIL THE FARRO in a medium saucepan of salted water until tender, about 30 to 40 minutes. Drain and cool completely. *(The farro can be cooked and refrigerated 1 day ahead.)*

Fry the bacon in a heavy large skillet over medium heat until crisp, turning occasionally. Using a slotted spoon, transfer the bacon to a paper towel or brown paper bag to drain. Add the walnuts to the same skillet and stir over medium heat until toasted, about 1 minute. Using a slotted spoon, transfer the walnuts to the paper towel with the bacon. Pour off all but 2 tablespoons of the bacon grease from the skillet. Return the skillet to medium heat. Add the farro and stir until lightly toasted and golden brown, about 4 minutes. Remove the skillet from the heat and let the farro cool while preparing the rest of the salad.

Whisk the oil, vinegar, garlic, and salt to blend in the bottom of a large bowl. Add the greens, pear, onion, dates, farro, and walnuts to the salad. Crumble the bacon over the salad; add the Parmesan shavings and season with freshly ground black pepper. Toss gently and serve.

ITALIAN CHOPPED SALAD

I like to serve this big chopped salad with large slices of grilled bread brushed with olive oil and rubbed with garlic—along with a fruity Italian wine, such as a Chianti Classico or Bardolino.

6 cups chopped romaine lettuce

1 small head radicchio, chopped

6 ounces diced sharp Italian cheese, such as Toscano, Piave, or sharp provolone (about 1 1/2 cups)

1 fennel bulb, trimmed and chopped

1 1/2 cups halved cherry tomatoes

6 ounces diced salami (about 1 1/2 cups)

1 (14-ounce) can garbanzo beans, rinsed and drained

1 red or green bell pepper, chopped

1 cup chopped red onion

1/2 cup coarsely chopped pitted oil-cured black olives

2/3 cups fresh basil leaves, torn into pieces

Oregano Vinaigrette (page 52)

IN A LARGE bowl, combine the romaine, radicchio, cheese, fennel, tomatoes, salami, garbanzo beans, red pepper, red onion, olives, and basil in a large bowl. Add enough of the Oregano Vinaigrette to season to taste and toss well.

FIG, FENNEL, AND BARLEY SALAD
with Bûcheron, Speck, and Honey-Spice Walnuts

This salad is pure fall bliss when figs are ripe and abundant. Speck is similar to prosciutto, but it is lightly smoked. Bûcheron is an aged goat cheese with a soft-ripening rind. Sold in rounds, it gets gooey on the edges and very flavorful as it ages. If you can't find Bûcheron, you can substitute any soft fresh goat cheese. Fig balsamic vinegar (which is used in the dressing) is a fig-infused, slightly thick balsamic that really enhances the figs in the salad—it's usually available at specialty foods stores, but any good-quality balsamic will do the trick.

BARLEY

1/2 cup pearl barley

DRESSING

3 tablespoons fig balsamic vinegar

1/4 cup finely chopped shallot

1 garlic clove, pressed

1 teaspoon minced fresh thyme

1/4 teaspoon kosher salt

6 tablespoons toasted walnut oil

SALAD

1 small head radicchio

5 cups mixed baby greens

1 small fennel bulb, trimmed, very thinly sliced

3 ounces thinly sliced speck or prosciutto, torn into strips

12 small ripe figs, cut in half

6 ounces Bûcheron cheese or other soft fresh goat cheese

3/4 cup Honey-Spice Glazed Walnuts (page 172)

RINSE THE BARLEY and combine it with 2 cups water in a heavy medium saucepan. Season the water generously with salt and boil until the barley is tender and the water is absorbed, about 30 minutes. Remove from the heat and let cool completely. *(Barley can be prepared up to 3 days ahead. Cover and refrigerate.)*

For the dressing: In a small bowl, combine the vinegar, shallot, garlic, thyme, and salt and whisk to blend. Gradually whisk in the oil and season with pepper.

For the salad: Remove the outer leaves of the radicchio and combine them with the salad greens in a large bowl. Finely chop the remaining head radicchio (you should have about 1/2 cup). In a medium bowl, mix the barley, fennel, and chopped radicchio with 1/4 cup of the dressing. Season the barley mixture to taste with salt and pepper.

Add enough of the dressing to the salad greens and radicchio to season to taste and toss to coat. Scatter the speck over the greens and top with the barley mixture. Garnish with the figs, cheese, and walnuts and serve.

Honey-Spice Glazed Walnuts

A hint of honey as well as pepper and allspice make these a wonderful addition to salads.

¼ cup (firmly packed) golden brown sugar

1 tablespoon honey

½ teaspoon kosher salt

¼ teaspoon ground allspice

¼ teaspoon freshly ground black pepper

2 cups walnut halves and pieces

LINE A LARGE sheet pan with parchment paper. Bring the brown sugar, 2 tablespoons water, the honey, salt, allspice, and pepper to a boil in a heavy large nonstick skillet over medium-high heat. Add the walnuts and stir with a silicone spatula until they are lightly toasted and the syrup mixture begins to darken and caramelize, about 3 minutes. Transfer the walnuts to the prepared sheet pan, separating them with a fork. Let the walnuts cool completely. *(Walnuts can be prepared up to 1 week ahead. Transfer to an airtight container and store at room temperature.)*

CROQUE MADAME DANS LE JARDIN

You might be thinking that this is just a classic French bistro sandwich served on a bed of greens—and you'd be right. But I've structured the open-face sandwich (*tartine*) to magically fall apart for easy eating with the crisp, tart greens.

SAUCE

1 tablespoon unsalted butter

2 tablespoons unbleached all-purpose flour

1 cup cold milk

1 bay leaf (preferably fresh)

¼ cup (packed) grated Gruyère cheese

Freshly grated nutmeg

TARTINES AND SALAD

4 slices pain au levain (crusty country-style French bread), lightly toasted

¾ cup (packed) grated Gruyère cheese

4 ounces thinly sliced smoked ham

1 tablespoon butter

4 eggs

8 cups mixed peppery greens, such as frisée, arugula, radicchio, red mustard, and chopped curly endive

Mustard-Shallot Vinaigrette (page 145)

FOR THE SAUCE: Melt the butter in a heavy small saucepan over medium heat. Add the flour and stir constantly 1 minute. (Do not brown the flour.) Add the milk all at once and the bay leaf. Whisk to combine. Stir the sauce until it thickens and just comes to a boil, about 1 minute. Remove from the heat and stir in the cheese and a light grating of fresh nutmeg. Let cool slightly. (*Can be prepared 3 days ahead; cover and refrigerate.*)

For the *tartines*: Preheat the broiler. Line a heavy large baking sheet with parchment. Working on a cutting board, spread 1 piece of toast with a layer of the sauce (about 1 generous tablespoonful). Sprinkle the sauce with 1 tablespoon of the cheese. Arrange a ham slice atop the cheese and spread a thick layer of the sauce over the ham. Sprinkle the tartine with 1 tablespoon of the cheese. Repeat with the remaining toast, sauce, cheese, and ham to make 4 tartines. Using a large sharp knife, cut the tartines into 1-inch squares. Carefully transfer the squares to the prepared baking sheet, reassembling the tartines. Broil until the cheese melts and a few brown spots appear.

Meanwhile, melt the butter in a heavy large well-seasoned cast-iron or nonstick skillet over medium heat. Crack the eggs into the skillet and fry until just set on the bottom, about 1 minute. Carefully place 1 egg atop each tartine on the baking sheet. Sprinkle the eggs with salt, pepper, and the remaining cheese. Broil until the cheese melts but the egg yolk is still runny.

In a large bowl, toss the greens with vinaigrette to taste and divide among 4 plates. Transfer the tartines to the center of the greens and serve with a fork and knife.

STEAKHOUSE SALAD

Here's a salad that combines favorites from your local steakhouse: steak (of course), crispy potatoes, and creamy blue cheese dressing. This is the first recipe that I developed for this book, as I wanted to assure my husband that the many months of salads that lay ahead did in no way mean interminable nights of "rabbit food."

1 tablespoon extra virgin olive oil, plus more for brushing

6 ounces fingerling potatoes, cut in half lengthwise

1 (8-ounce) steak (about 1 inch thick), such as strip, top sirloin, or rib-eye

1 large garlic clove, pressed

Lettuce leaves to line plates (about 8), such as green or red leaf, or oakleaf lettuce

2 tomatoes, cut into 6 wedges

Creamy Blue Cheese Dressing (page 135)

2 green onions, thinly sliced

HEAT 1 TABLESPOON olive oil in a heavy medium skillet over medium-high heat. Add the potatoes, cut side down. Cook the potatoes until browned on the bottoms, about 5 minutes. Turn them and sprinkle with salt. Reduce the heat to medium and continue to cook until the potatoes are browned and tender, about 8 minutes. Turn the potatoes and remove the skillet from the heat.

Meanwhile, prepare a grill to medium heat or heat a large cast-iron skillet over medium-high heat. Brush both sides of the steak with olive oil and rub with the garlic. Sprinkle the steak with salt and pepper. Grill or fry the steak until well browned, about 4 minutes per side for medium-rare. Let the steaks rest while preparing the salads.

Line 2 plates with the lettuce leaves. Arrange the tomatoes and potatoes over the lettuce, dividing evenly. Thinly slice the steak and divide the steak between plates. Spoon about 2 tablespoons of the Creamy Blue Cheese Dressing over each salad and sprinkle with the green onions. Serve, passing additional dressing separately

SALADS WITH MEAT   175

ARGENTINE GRILLED STEAK AND VEGETABLE SALAD with Chimichurri Vinaigrette

Use thin grass-fed steaks to best approximate a gaucho *churrasco*.

CHIMICHURRI VINAIGRETTE

¼ cup finely chopped shallot

1 bay leaf

⅓ cup extra virgin olive oil

4 garlic cloves, minced

½ teaspoon crushed red pepper

3 tablespoons finely chopped fresh Italian parsley

3 tablespoons red wine vinegar

1 tablespoon finely chopped fresh oregano

½ teaspoon kosher salt

SALAD

1½ pounds steaks (each about ½-inch thick), such as grass-fed rib-eye or strip steaks

Extra virgin olive oil

1 teaspoon smoked paprika

1 teaspoon kosher salt

4 small-to-medium zucchini, quartered lengthwise

2 large red bell peppers, cut into ½- to ¾-inch-wide strips

1 medium red onion, cut into ½-inch-thick rounds

4 cups arugula

FOR THE VINAIGRETTE: Combine the shallot and bay leaf in a medium bowl. Heat the olive oil, garlic, and crushed red pepper in a heavy large skillet over medium-high heat until the garlic softens slightly but does not brown, about 1 minute. Immediately pour the oil mixture over the shallot and bay leaf in the bowl and let stand until cool. Stir in the parsley, vinegar, oregano, and salt.

For the salad: Prepare a grill to medium-high heat. Rub both sides of the steak with olive oil, as well as the paprika and kosher salt. Season both sides with freshly ground black pepper. Lightly brush the zucchini, red peppers, and red onion rounds with olive oil. Grill the vegetables until browned and tender, turning occasionally, about 8 minutes. Transfer them all to a plate. Grill the steak until well browned on both sides, turning once, about 6 minutes for medium-rare. Transfer the steaks to a plate and let stand while preparing the rest of the salad.

Divide the arugula leaves among 4 plates, arranging attractively. Top the arugula with the room-temperature zucchini, red peppers, and red onions, dividing evenly. Transfer the steak to a cutting board and cut crosswise into thin strips. Arrange the warm steak atop the vegetables, dividing evenly. Drizzle any steak juices from the plate over the steaks and the salads, dividing evenly. Spoon some chimichurri vinaigrette over the steaks. Serve with additional chimichurri.

KOREAN BARBECUE BEEF SALAD

If short on time, you can buy Korean kalbi marinade and use ½ cup of it in place of the marinade below. This salad follows the "healthy heart" guidelines of just 4 ounces of meat protein per person, *but,* if you love this kind of beef and want to splurge, you can double the amount of beef and marinade. Kimchee is a traditional relish for Korean food. If you like the spicy fermented cabbage or radish condiment, go ahead and serve it with the salad. I like to eat this salad wrapped in the large lettuce leaves with my hands—it's sort of messy, but extra tasty. Instead of bread, steamed rice rounds out this meal nicely—it can be rolled inside the lettuce leaves with the beef. Remember to allow for the 4 hours of marinating before grilling the beef.

BEEF

¼ cup (packed) golden brown sugar

¼ cup soy sauce

1 tablespoon rice wine vinegar

1 tablespoon roasted sesame seeds

1 tablespoon toasted sesame oil

1 garlic clove, minced

1 teaspoon finely grated peeled fresh ginger

¼ teaspoon crushed red pepper

1 pound top sirloin steak, cut crosswise into ¼-inch strips

SALAD

3 tablespoons rice wine vinegar

2 tablespoons toasted sesame oil

1½ tablespoons soy sauce

1 tablespoon (packed) golden brown sugar

1 garlic clove, minced or pressed

1 teaspoon finely grated peeled fresh ginger

4 cups thinly sliced napa cabbage

8 ounces (about 3 cups) bean sprouts

6 green onions, thinly sliced on a diagonal

2 tablespoons roasted sesame seeds

8 leaves green leaf lettuce

Purchased kimchee (optional)

FOR THE BEEF: Stir the first 8 ingredients to blend in an 8-inch square baking dish. Add the beef and stir to coat. Cover and refrigerate 4 hours or overnight.

For the salad: Prepare a grill to medium heat. In a large bowl, combine the first 6 ingredients and whisk to blend. Add the cabbage, bean sprouts, green onions, and sesame seeds to the rice vinegar mixture in the large bowl and toss to combine. Arrange 2 of the lettuce leaves on each of 4 plates. Arrange the cabbage mixture atop the lettuce leaves, dividing evenly.

Grill the beef until browned and cooked through, turning once, about 4 minutes.

Top the cabbage mixture with the beef, dividing evenly. Spoon some kimchee alongside if desired, and serve.

CARIBBEAN SALAD with Jerk Pork

Owing to the array of jewel-tone fruits and fluffy greens that accent the tenderloin, my daughters dubbed this composed salad "lady pork." But given the thick slices of spicy meat, most men would be content to make a meal of it. "Jerk," by the way, is the traditional Jamaican citrus-and-spice rub and marinade, not someone who thinks this salad is too pretty to eat for dinner. A *supreme* is a segment of citrus that has been carefully denuded of peel, pith, membranes, and seeds.

PORK

1 pork tenderloin (about 1¼ pounds)

1 generous tablespoon salt-free Jamaican-blend jerk seasoning (such as Spice Hunter)

1 tablespoon extra virgin olive oil

DRESSING

¼ cup extra virgin olive oil

2 tablespoons freshly squeezed lime juice

2 tablespoons orange juice

2 teaspoons golden brown sugar

1 teaspoon salt-free Jamaican blend jerk seasoning

1 garlic clove, pressed

½ teaspoon kosher salt

SALAD

8 cups butter lettuce (about 1 large or 2 small heads), torn into 3-inch pieces

4 cups arugula, torn (if necessary) into 3-inch pieces

1 small red bell pepper, cut into thin, 2-inch-long slices

¼ red onion, thinly sliced

1 ripe mango, peeled, pitted, and sliced

2 oranges, peeled and sliced into rounds

1 large firm-ripe avocado, peeled, pitted, and sliced

1 grapefruit, cut into supremes (page 131)

FOR THE PORK: Preheat the oven to 350°F. Sprinkle the tenderloin generously with salt and the jerk seasoning, coating evenly. Heat the olive oil in a heavy large ovenproof skillet over medium-high heat. Add the pork and cook until just browned on all sides, turning occasionally, about 4 minutes. Transfer the skillet to the oven and roast the pork until an instant-read thermometer registers 140°F when inserted into the thickest part of the pork, about 15 minutes. Transfer the pork to a cutting board and let stand while preparing the salad.

For the dressing: Whisk all the ingredients to blend in a small bowl.

For the salad: In a large bowl, combine the lettuce, arugula, bell pepper, and onion. Add 2 or 3 tablespoons of the dressing to coat, season the lettuce mixture to taste with salt and pepper, and toss well. Divide the lettuce mixture among 4 plates. Top it with the mango, orange, avocado, and grapefruit, dividing evenly. Thinly slice the pork and arrange atop each salad, dividing evenly. Rewhisk the remaining dressing and spoon over the salads; serve.

ROAST BEEF with Red Leaf Lettuce, Red Onions, Radishes, and Horseradish Cream

This is the type of salad you might serve your grandpa when he is visiting in the summer—deli slices of cold roast beef with a creamy kick of horseradish dressing and the peppery crunch of radishes—it's sort of old-fashioned, but it's also cool and smart on a hot day or night.

Red leaf lettuce to line plates, such as red oakleaf (about 1 head separated into leaves)

12 ounces thinly sliced rare roast beef

1 bunch radishes, trimmed and sliced into rounds

½ small red onion, cut into very thin rounds

Horseradish Cream (page 99)

1 tablespoon whole grain mustard

Cornichons or gherkins (optional)

LINE EACH OF 4 salad plates with the lettuce leaves. Roll the slices of roast beef attractively and arrange atop the greens. Scatter the radishes and the red onion over the beef. Stir the mustard into the Horseradish Cream Dressing. Spoon the dressing over the salads, garnish with cornichons, and serve.

THAI-STYLE GRILLED BEEF SALAD

This salad is light with bright, clear flavors. If you have cold leftover steak from a restaurant or barbecue, go ahead and use it, thinly sliced, in place of the freshly grilled beef. For convenience, the steak can marinate overnight.

Thai Dressing (page 139)

1 large garlic clove, pressed

1 teaspoon chili-garlic sauce

1 (1- to 1¼-pound) top sirloin steak

4 ounces (½ package) brown rice pad thai noodles

Butter lettuce (about 1 head) to line plates

2 kaffir lime leaves, cut into slivers (optional)

4 small tomatoes, cut into wedges

1 cucumber, peeled and thinly sliced

2 green onions, thinly sliced

¼ cup mint leaves

2 tablespoons chopped fresh basil, preferably Thai basil

2 tablespoons chopped fresh cilantro

COMBINE 2 TABLESPOONS of the Thai Dressing with the garlic and chili-garlic sauce in a small baking dish. Add the steak and turn to coat. Let the steak marinate up to 1 hour at room temperature or overnight in the refrigerator.

Cook the noodles in a large saucepan of rapidly boiling salted water until tender, about 2 minutes. Drain the noodles and transfer to a bowl of cold water to cool.

Prepare a grill to medium heat or heat a large cast-iron skillet over medium-high heat. Grill or fry the steak until well browned, about 4 minutes per side for medium-rare. Let the steak rest at room temperature 5 to 15 minutes.

Line each of 4 plates with the butter lettuce leaves. In a large bowl, toss the noodles with 2 tablespoons of the Thai Dressing and the lime leaves, if using. Divide the cold noodles among the lettuce-lined plates. Thinly slice the steak. Arrange the hot steak slices atop the noodles, dividing evenly. Garnish the salads with the tomatoes and cucumber slices. Sprinkle the salads with the green onions, mint, basil, and cilantro, dividing evenly. Spoon about 1 tablespoon dressing over each salad and serve, passing the remaining dressing separately.

VIETNAMESE PORK MEATBALL BANH MI SALAD

A banh mi is a Franco-Vietnamese hybrid sandwich often made with pork meatballs. Here, the components are deconstructed and served as a fun and satisfying salad that's great for lunch or a casual dinner. It's really great with beer and a soft baguette. Daikon is a smooth, white, and very large (sometimes over a foot long) Asian radish. It's available at most supermarkets. The spicy mayo that gets drizzled over the salad is a multipurpose condiment that tastes great spread on most sandwiches.

SPICY MAYO

⅓ cup Coffe-mug Mayo (page 183) or prepared mayonnaise

½ green onion, finely chopped

1 tablespoon sriracha sauce

PICKLED VEGETABLES

1 cup grated peeled carrot

1 cup grated peeled daikon radish

2 tablespoons rice vinegar

2 tablespoons sugar

½ teaspoon kosher salt

MEATBALLS

1 pound ground pork

3 green onions, finely chopped

4 garlic cloves, peeled and finely minced

¼ cup finely chopped fresh basil

2 tablespoons minced fresh cilantro

1 tablespoon Vietnamese or Thai fish sauce (*nuoc nam* or *nam pla*)

1 tablespoon sriracha sauce

1 tablespoon sugar

2 teaspoons cornstarch

1 teaspoon freshly ground black pepper

1 teaspoon kosher salt

1 tablespoon toasted sesame oil

8 leaves (about 1 head) red leaf lettuce

1 Persian or pickling cucumber, thinly sliced, or ½ hothouse cucumber, thinly sliced

½ cup fresh cilantro sprigs

1 jalapeño pepper, thinly sliced

FOR THE SPICY mayo: Stir all the ingredients to blend in a small bowl. *(Mayo can be prepared 4 days ahead; cover and refrigerate.)*

For the pickled vegetables: Stir all the ingredients to blend in a small bowl. Let stand 1 hour or cover and refrigerate overnight.

For the meatballs: Combine the pork and the next 10 ingredients in a large bowl. Blend well. Roll the meat into 1-inch balls and arrange in a single layer in a baking dish. *(Meatballs can be made 1 day ahead. Cover with plastic wrap and refrigerate.)*

Heat the sesame oil in a very large heavy skillet over medium-high heat. Add the meatballs to the skillet (avoid crowding them or cook them in batches to prevent them from steaming) and reduce the heat to medium. Cook meatballs until well browned and cooked through, turning frequently, about 15 minutes.

Arrange 2 lettuce leaves on each of 4 plates. Drain the pickled vegetables and arrange them atop the lettuce leaves, dividing evenly. Scatter the cucumber slices over the lettuce leaves and top with the hot meatballs, dividing evenly. Garnish the salads with the cilantro and the jalapeño slices. Drizzle a small amount of the spicy mayo over the salads and serve.

Coffee-mug Mayo

MAKES ½ CUP

I've watched French women make mayonnaise in a teacup, without any measurements and using only a fork. The key to success is confidence (which French women have in spades) and LOTS of mustard—which helps to emulsify the mix. I prefer to use a mug and a small whisk, but you can opt for a small, deep bowl, or a large teacup and fork if you prefer.

1 egg yolk

1 tablespoon Dijon mustard

¼ cup canola oil

2 tablespoons extra virgin olive oil

1 teaspoon freshly squeezed lemon juice

USING A SMALL whisk or fork, stir the egg yolk and mustard vigorously in a large mug or small, deep bowl. Combine both oils in a small measuring cup. Drizzle about 2 teaspoons of the oil mixture over the egg mixture in the mug and whisk vigorously, about 30 seconds. Repeat 2 more times. Slowly add the remaining oil mixture to the egg mixture in the mug, pouring it in a slow, steady stream while whisking constantly, continuing to whisk until mayonnaise thickens to spreadable consistency. Whisk in the lemon juice and season to taste with salt and pepper.

AIOLI VERSION

Use extra virgin olive oil for both the oils and stir in 2 pressed garlic cloves.

MUSTARD-HERB VERSION

Increase the mustard to 2 tablespoons and stir in 1 tablespoon minced fresh herbs.

RED PEPPER VERSION

Stir in 1 tablespoon sriracha hot sauce and 1 pressed garlic clove.

GRILLED PORK AND GREEN ONIONS
with Romesco Sauce, Greens, and Sherry Vinaigrette

Robust flavors combine in this salad that celebrates the Spanish spring tradition of feasting on grilled green onions with romesco—a sauce made with roasted red peppers, almonds, olive oil, and garlic. For convenience, the pork can marinate overnight.

PORK

1 pork tenderloin (about 1¼ pounds)

Extra virgin olive oil

3 garlic cloves, minced or pressed

2 teaspoons smoked paprika

1 teaspoon kosher salt

SHERRY VINAIGRETTE

2 tablespoons sherry vinegar

1 garlic clove, pressed

½ teaspoon brown sugar

½ teaspoon kosher salt

⅓ cup extra virgin olive oil

SALAD

Extra virgin olive oil

12 ounces small fingering or other spring potatoes, cut in half lengthwise

8 green onions, trimmed

6 cups mixed greens

Romesco Sauce (opposite) for serving

FOR THE PORK: Rub the pork with olive oil, the garlic, smoked paprika, and kosher salt. Cover and let stand up to 1 hour at room temperature or overnight in the refrigerator.

For the vinaigrette: Whisk the vinegar, garlic, sugar, and salt to blend in a small bowl. Gradually whisk in the olive oil.

For the salad: Set two 24-inch pieces of aluminum foil on a work surface, forming a cross. Drizzle the center of the foil with olive oil. Arrange the potatoes, cut side down, in the center. Sprinkle the potatoes with salt and pepper. Enclose the potatoes in the foil, sealing carefully so that they are in a single layer and the packet measures about 8 inches square.

Preheat a grill to medium-high heat. Place the potato packet on the grill so that the cut sides of the potatoes are facing down. Place the pork alongside the potatoes and cook until the potatoes are tender when pierced with a long thin skewer and the pork registers 145°F on an instant-read thermometer inserted into the thickest part of the tenderloin, about 25 minutes. Transfer the pork to a cutting board and remove the potato packet from the heat. (Maintain grill temperature.) Brush the green onions lightly with olive oil. Grill the onions until lightly browned and tender, about 1 minute per side.

Toss the greens with enough vinaigrette to coat lightly. Arrange the greens on a platter or divide among 4 plates. Slice the pork. Arrange the warm pork, potatoes, and green onions atop the greens. Serve the salads with Romesco Sauce.

Romesco Sauce

Piquillo peppers are sweet red beak-shaped chiles from northern Spain. The peppers are roasted and sold in jars at gourmet food stores. If you can't find the slightly more robustly flavored piquillos, you can substitute an equal amount of jarred roasted red peppers with very fine results. Romesco is wonderful on any grilled meat, poultry, or fish.

1 (10.4-ounce) jar piquillo peppers, drained

½ cup almonds, toasted

¼ cup extra virgin olive oil

3 garlic cloves

2 teaspoons smoked paprika

½ teaspoon kosher salt

PURÉE ALL THE ingredients in a blender until smooth. Season with additional salt to taste. (*Romesco Sauce can be prepared up to 3 days ahead. Transfer to a small plastic container and refrigerate.*)

OAKLEAF LETTUCE with Grilled Pork, Corn, and Nectarines with Honey-Marjoram Vinaigrette

Grilling brings out the flavor and sweetness of the corn and nectarines. Peaches, plums, or pluots are also good in this salad.

1 pound (³/₄-inch-thick) boneless pork loin chops (about 2)

Extra virgin olive oil

3 ears corn, shucked

6 small nectarines, peaches, plums, or pluots, cut in half and pitted

12 cups red or green oakleaf or other loose-leaf lettuce

1/2 small red onion, thinly sliced

Honey-Marjoram Vinaigrette (opposite)

PREHEAT A GRILL to medium-high heat.

Place the pork in a medium baking dish, drizzle lightly with olive oil, and turn to coat. Brush the corn and nectarines with olive oil.

Grill the corn until browned in bits on all sides, turning occasionally, about 8 minutes. Let the corn cool and maintain the grill at medium-high heat.

Hold the corn perpendicular to a cutting board and using a large sharp knife, cut the kernels from the cob.

In a large bowl, combine the corn kernels, lettuce, and red onion.

Season both sides of the pork with salt and pepper. Grill the pork and the nectarines until the pork is browned on both sides and cooked to medium and the nectarines are lightly charred and tender on both sides, about 8 minutes. Transfer the pork to a cutting board and let stand 5 minutes.

Toss the lettuce mixture with enough Honey-Marjoram Vinaigrette to coat the lettuce and season the salad to taste with salt and pepper. Divide the lettuce mixture among 4 plates. Thinly slice the pork and divide the slices among the salads. Arrange the nectarines atop the salads, dividing evenly. Drizzle the pork and nectarines with the remaining vinaigrette and serve.

Honey-Marjoram Vinaigrette

Marjoram is one of my favorite herbs. It has a sweet, piney menthol flavor that enhances all manner of foods.

3 tablespoons white balsamic vinegar

$1\frac{1}{2}$ tablespoons red wine vinegar

1 tablespoon chopped fresh marjoram leaves

2 teaspoons honey

$1\frac{1}{2}$ teaspoons Dijon mustard

1 garlic clove, pressed

$\frac{1}{2}$ teaspoon kosher salt

6 tablespoons extra virgin olive oil

IN A SMALL bowl, combine both vinegars and the marjoram and stir to blend; let stand 15 minutes. Mix in the honey, mustard, garlic, and salt. Gradually whisk in the olive oil. Season the vinaigrette with freshly ground black pepper.

TRIO OF GRATED SALADS
with Hearty Greens and Pan-Seared Sausages

Salades râpées—grated vegetable salads—are popular as starters at French bistros. When combined with succulent sausages and hearty greens, all that you need is a glass of *vin rouge* and a baguette and you've got *un dîner super.*

Roasted Beets (page 56)

Mustard-Shallot Vinaigrette (page 145)

2 tablespoons minced fresh parsley, divided

1 pound (about 4 large) carrots, peeled and grated

1 teaspoon minced fresh thyme leaves, divided

1 pound (about 1 medium) celery root, peeled and grated

2 tablespoons sour cream

2 teaspoons Dijon mustard

1 tablespoon extra virgin olive oil

6 fresh sausages, such as French garlic, Italian, or bratwurst

10 cups mixed peppery greens, such as frisée, arugula, radicchio, red mustard, and chopped curly endive

1½ tablespoons red wine vinegar

PEEL THE BEETS and thinly slice. Stack the beet slices and cut them crosswise into thin strips (you should have about 2⅔ cups). Combine the beets in a medium bowl with 2 tablespoons of the Mustard-Shallot Vinaigrette and 2 teaspoons of the chopped parsley. Season the beet salad with salt and freshly ground black pepper.

In another medium bowl, combine the carrots with 3 tablespoons of the vinaigrette, 2 teaspoons of the chopped parsley and ½ teaspoon minced thyme. Season the carrots to taste with salt and pepper.

In a separate medium bowl, combine the celery root with the remaining vinaigrette (about 3 tablespoons), remaining 2 teaspoons chopped parsley, and the remaining ½ teaspoon minced thyme. Add the sour cream and mustard and mix well. Season the salad to taste with salt and pepper. *(The salads can be prepared 1 day ahead. Cover and refrigerate separately.)*

Heat the olive oil in a heavy large skillet over medium heat. Add the sausages and fry, turning them frequently, until they are well browned and cooked through, about 12 minutes. Meanwhile, arrange the greens on 6 plates, dividing evenly. Top the greens with the hot sausages, dividing evenly. Add the vinegar to the skillet and bring the vinegar just to a simmer. Drizzle the pan drippings evenly over the sausages and greens. Spoon the grated salads alongside the sausages and serve.

LAMB RIB CHOPS
with Cracked Wheat, Mint, and Asian Apple Pear Salad

Bulgur, or cracked wheat, is the grain that stars in tabouli, the parsley, wheat, and tomato salad that is so popular in the Middle East. Here, the cracked wheat takes on a sweeter tone with crunchy Asian apple pear and mint leaves. Bulgur is available at many supermarkets; Bob's Red Mill is a very good brand. Asian apple pears are cousins of our pears—they are the color of Bosc pears with a round, apple shape and apple crispness, but are even juicier, like a pear. Apple pears are not as exotic as they sound, as they are available year-round at most supermarkets. The salad is lovely on its own, but when paired with lamb rib chops, it makes a special and satisfying meal.

SALAD

1 cup whole grain quick-cooking bulgur wheat

1 (12-ounce) Asian apple pear, peeled, cored, and diced

1/2 cup chopped fresh mint

2 green onions, thinly sliced

1/4 cup (packed) coarsely chopped fresh Italian parsley

2 tablespoons pine nuts, toasted

1/3 cup extra virgin olive oil

3 tablespoons freshly squeezed lemon juice

2 garlic cloves, pressed

1/2 teaspoon kosher salt

LAMB

1 to 1 1/4 pounds lamb rib rack, frenched

Extra virgin olive oil

1 garlic clove, pressed

1 teaspoon ground coriander

1/2 teaspoon finely grated lemon peel

1/2 teaspoon kosher salt

2 tablespoons freshly squeezed lemon juice

1 tablespoon honey

About 8 large red lettuce leaves to line a platter or 4 plates

FOR THE SALAD: Place the bulgur in a large bowl; pour 1 cup boiling water over it and let stand until the bulgur is tender and the liquid is absorbed, about 1 hour.

Add the apple pear, mint, green onions, parsley, and pine nuts to the bulgur and toss well. In a small bowl, combine the olive oil, lemon juice, garlic, and salt and whisk to blend for the dressing. Spoon all but 2 tablespoons of the dressing over the bulgur salad and toss well. Season the salad to taste with additional salt and freshly ground black pepper.

For the lamb: Preheat the oven to 450°F. Brush a small roasting pan lightly with olive oil. Place the lamb rack in the prepared pan and rub with the garlic, coriander, lemon peel, and salt. Sprinkle the lamb with freshly ground black pepper. Roast the lamb in the oven until an instant-read thermometer inserted into the thickest part of the lamb registers 125°F, about 15 minutes. Transfer the lamb to a cutting board.

Set the roasting pan on the stovetop over medium-high heat. Add 3 tablespoons water, the lemon juice, and honey to the roasting pan and boil, stirring up any browned bits from the bottom of the pan until the liquid is reduced by half, about 2 minutes.

Line 4 plates or a platter with the red lettuce leaves. Drizzle the remaining 2 tablespoons dressing over the lettuce. Spoon the salad onto the center of the platter or plates. Slice the lamb into chops and surround the salad with the rib chops. Drizzle the lamb with the pan juices and serve.

Party Salads

MOST LADIES I KNOW HAVE BEEN TO QUITE A FEW BRIDAL AND BABY SHOW-ers and luncheons where the hostess serves chicken salad and fruit salad. In fact, I financed my entire culinary education in France whipping up chicken salads, seasonal fruit compotes, and lemon tarts for my mother's and her friends' various showers and luncheons. What's not to like about the menu? Both salads can be made ahead and are crowd pleasers—qualities desired for every party, not just one for ladies. While the salads in this book are "stand-alone" meals (with some being lighter than others), when entertaining, designing a menu around two or more salads is an easy and colorful way to serve a group. You could make any of the chicken salads in this book and throw in a bowl of diced fruit and call it a party, but there are so many other great ways to build a menu with salads.

When mixing and matching salads for parties, it's a good idea to keep balance, texture, seasonality, and preparation in mind. When pairing just two salads, I usually serve a do-ahead salad with a greens-based salad. Paella Salad pairs beautifully with Spanish Chopped Salad with Migas. Freekeh Salad with Apricots, Grilled Halloumi, and Zucchini is a great make-ahead grain-based salad that can be enjoyed with the Spinach Salad with Grilled Shrimp and Peppers at a casual get-together or with the Grilled Kale with Lamb and Garlic- Yogurt Dressing at a more formal soirée.

For some gatherings, a dinner served in courses is a focused way to eat salad. Following artfully arranged plates of Sardine-Stuffed Piquillo Peppers with Lemony Greens and Whole-Wheat Croutons with the Kale Salad with Wheat Berries, Parmesan, Pine Nuts, and Currants is a superlative way to ring in the fall. A first course of Roasted Tomato Salad with Arugula and Fromage Chacun à son Goût succeeded by Oakleaf Lettuce with Grilled Pork, Corn, and Nectarines with Honey-Marjoram Vinaigrette is a delight on a summer evening. With both combinations, I might cut down on the greens in the first course slightly.

For large parties, salads can be mixed and matched and recipes can be doubled or tripled. When serving several salads, be sure to select recipes without too many repeat ingredients. One way to go about selecting salads is to cook with ingredients that are in season. Summertime Corn and Ham Salad; Baby Octopus and White Bean Salad; Grilled Eggplant Salad with Heirloom Tomatoes, Fresh Mozzarella, and Pesto Vinaigrette; and Roasted Balsamic Chicken and Green Bean Salad with Goat Cheese in summer. Or go with a theme like a Pan-Asian menu of Chinese-Style Chicken Salad with Tangerines; Toasted Barley, Long Bean, and Shiitake Mushroom Salad with Teriyaki Tofu; Singapore-Style Chinese New Year Raw Fish "Tossed" Salad; and Vietnamese Pork Meatball Banh Mi Salad. Whatever the menu, keep in mind that people will sample just some of each salad, so a salad that serves four might serve eight when other salads tempt.

FATTOUSH SALAD with Lamb

Fattoush is a Levantine bread salad made with crunchy pita chips, garlicky dressing, crisp vegetables, and fresh herbs. Add a little freshly roasted or leftover lamb, or even a take-out kebab, and the side salad becomes a stunning lunch or dinner. Sumac is a spice made from the ground berries of the sumac bush. It has a tart-sweet flavor. Find sumac at Middle Eastern markets and online at Penzeys. Sumac and purslane add a lemony punch to the fattoush, but the salad is equally good—and authentic—served with an extra lemon wedge instead. Vegetarians can enjoy this salad with a hefty sprinkling of crumbled feta cheese instead of the lamb.

2 (9-inch) or 3 (6-inch) pita bread rounds

Extra virgin olive oil

1 generous teaspoon ground sumac (optional)

¼ teaspoon kosher salt

6 cups romaine lettuce, torn into bite-sized pieces

6 cups arugula, torn if necessary into bite-sized pieces

1 bunch radishes, trimmed and sliced

1½ cups cherry tomatoes, cut in half

2 Persian cucumbers, sliced

1 cup purslane leaves (from about 2 bunches; optional)

½ cup coarsely chopped fresh Italian parsley

Mediterranean Lemon Dressing (page 196)

Grilled Lamb Kebabs (page 196) or 1½ to 2 pounds thinly sliced leftover grilled or roasted lamb

½ cup fresh mint leaves

PREHEAT THE OVEN to 375°F.

Split the rounds of pita bread in half horizontally. Brush the split sides (the rough sides) with olive oil. Stack the rounds and cut them into 1½-inch squares. Spread the squares out on a large heavy baking sheet. Sprinkle the pita with the sumac, if using, and the salt. Bake the pita squares until crisp and golden brown, stirring once, about 10 minutes. Remove from the oven and let cool. (*Pita chips can be prepared up to 3 days ahead. Store them in an airtight container at room temperature.*)

Combine the romaine and the next 6 ingredients in a large bowl. Add the pita chips and enough Mediterranean Lemon Dressing to season to taste and toss well. Divide the salad among 6 plates and top with the lamb kebabs. Sprinkle the salads with the mint leaves and serve.

Mediterranean Lemon Dressing

Tahini is a sesame seed paste similar in texture to peanut butter. A touch of it adds a hint of nutty flavor and a creamy consistency to the dressing. Most people are familiar with tahini as an addition to hummus. Look for it at Middle Eastern markets and health foods stores.

1 tablespoon tahini

2 large garlic cloves, pressed

½ teaspoon kosher salt

¼ cup freshly squeezed lemon juice

⅓ cup extra virgin olive oil

COMBINE THE TAHINI, garlic, and salt in a medium bowl. Gradually whisk in the lemon juice, then the olive oil. *(Dressing can be made 1 week ahead. Cover and refrigerate.)*

Grilled Lamb Kebabs

Marinated and grilled lamb is a super addition to the Fattoush Salad. For the tenderest kebabs, be sure to use lamb meat that has been very well trimmed. If you ask nicely, the butcher will do this for you.

2 tablespoons extra virgin olive oil, plus more for brushing

3 garlic cloves, pressed

1 teaspoon ground cumin

1 teaspoon kosher salt

1 teaspoon dried marjoram

1 teaspoon paprika

½ teaspoon freshly ground black pepper

2 pounds well-trimmed boneless leg of lamb, cut into 1½-inch cubes

6 metal skewers

IN A LARGE bowl, combine the first 7 ingredients and whisk to blend. Add the lamb and stir to coat with the garlic mixture. Cover and let the lamb stand 20 minutes at room temperature or overnight in the refrigerator.

Prepare a grill to medium-high heat. Thread the lamb onto skewers, dividing evenly. Brush the kebabs with olive oil. Grill the kebabs until the lamb is well browned but pink on the inside, turning occasionally, 7 to 9 minutes for medium-rare.

GRILLED KALE
with Lamb and Garlic-Mint Yogurt Dressing

Hearty and tender yet chewy with a slight smoky char, grilled kale is a revelation. With a prelude of hummus and pita, this is a great dish to serve to mixed company—carnivores and vegetarians—as meat eaters will love the juicy lamb and vegetarians can make a meal with the kale, yogurt, and thick slices of olive bread. I call for Russian kale in this recipe because it's not as curly as regular kale. The curly variety tends to burn when the frilly edge of the leaf gets too close to the fire.

GARLIC-MINT YOGURT DRESSING

1 cup whole milk or 2% plain yogurt

3 tablespoons extra virgin olive oil

1/3 cup chopped fresh mint

1 teaspoon (scant) kosher salt

2 garlic cloves, pressed

LAMB AND KALE

2 lamb rib racks

5 tablespoons extra virgin olive oil, divided

2 large garlic cloves, minced or pressed

2 pounds (about 2 bunches) Russian or lacinato kale, stems trimmed

2 tablespoons chopped fresh mint

FOR THE DRESSING: Combine all the ingredients in a medium bowl and whisk to blend. *(Dressing can be prepared 1 day ahead; cover and refrigerate.)*

For the lamb and the kale: Using a sharp thin knife, cut between the ribs to create rib chops. Combine the lamb chops, 2 tablespoons olive oil, and the garlic in a large baking dish and turn to coat.

Place the kale in a large bowl and drizzle with the remaining 3 tablespoons olive oil. Using your hands, rub the olive oil over both sides of the kale leaves until lightly coated.

Prepare a grill to medium heat. Working in batches, arrange the kale leaves in a single layer on the grill and cook until just wilted, about 30 seconds to 1 minute. Turn the kale and cook until the leaves are tender and very lightly charred at the edges, about 30 seconds to 1 minute longer. (Some of the leaves may not need turning, depending on the heat of the grill.) Transfer the kale to a large platter. Grill the lamb until just browned on both sides, turning once, about 4 minutes for medium-rare.

Arrange the lamb chops atop the kale. Spoon the yogurt dressing over the lamb. Sprinkle the salad with the mint leaves and serve.

ONE SWEET FINISH
Chocolate Cream Pie

| MAKES 1 PIE; ABOUT 10 SERVINGS

I wanted to include one fantastic sweet in this book because, when you eat salad for lunch or dinner, shouldn't you be rewarded with dessert? This is a decadent pie, and while it can be carved into about ten attractive wedges, a tiny sliver might just be enough for some. The pie can be made ahead, but I prefer to top it with whipped cream just before serving. If desired, you can slice the pie and serve it with a spoonful of whipped cream alongside.

CRUST

3/4 cup unbleached all-purpose flour

1/2 cup whole raw almonds, toasted and finely chopped

6 tablespoons sugar

1/4 cup natural unsweetened cocoa powder

1/2 teaspoon kosher salt

6 tablespoons unsalted butter, melted and cooled slightly

FILLING

2/3 cup sugar

1/4 cup cornstarch

2 tablespoons natural unsweetened cocoa powder

1/4 teaspoon kosher salt

4 large egg yolks

3 cups milk (I use 2%)

8 ounces bittersweet chocolate (54 to 60% cacao), chopped

1 tablespoon dark rum

TOPPING

1 cup chilled whipping cream

2 tablespoons sugar

1/2 teaspoon vanilla extract

FOR THE CRUST: Preheat the oven to 375°F. Butter a 9-inch pie dish or pan.

Combine the flour, almonds, sugar, cocoa powder, and salt in a medium bowl. Using a fork, stir in the butter until the mixture resembles moist sand. Press the dough firmly and evenly over the bottom and up the sides of the pie dish. Bake the crust until just browned at the edges, about 11 minutes. Let the crust cool completely.

For the filling: In a heavy large saucepan, combine the sugar, cornstarch, cocoa powder, and salt and whisk to blend. Beat in the egg yolks. Gradually whisk in the milk. Whisk the filling over medium-high heat until the mixture thickens and boils, about 1 minute. Remove the filling from the heat and immediately stir in the chocolate, whisking until the chocolate melts and the filling is smooth. Stir in the rum. Pour the filling into the crust and smooth the top. Let the pie cool to room temperature and cover loosely with waxed paper. Chill the pie until cold, at least 2 hours or overnight.

For the topping: Beat the cream, sugar, and vanilla in a large bowl until firm peaks form. Spread the topping over the pie and serve.

Index

Page references in italic refer to illustrations.

A

Acorn Squash, Roasted Brussels Sprout and, Salad with Quinoa, Pepitas, and Pomegranates, *40*, 41–42

aioli:
Saffron, *102*, 104
Version of Coffee-Mug Mayo, 183

almonds, 28
Marcona, Roasted Beet and Blood Orange Salad with Goat Cheese and, *54*, 55–56
Romesco Sauce, 185
Spanish Chopped Salad with Migas, *162*, 163

amaranth, 12

Ancho-Lime Vinaigrette, 39

anchovy:
Caesar Dressing, 126
Vinaigrette, 94
White, Potato, and Parsley Salad, 91

apricots:
Freekeh Salad with Grilled Haloumi, Zucchini and, 78, *79*
Smoked Duck Salad with Haricots Verts, Pistachios and, 147

Argentine Grilled Steak and Vegetable Salad with Chimichurri Vinaigrette, 176

Artichoke, Grilled Baby, and Asparagus Salad with Shrimp and Saffron Aioli, *102*, 103–4

arugula, 10, 12, 21
and Bresaola Salad with Parmesan Shavings and Lemon-Chive Drizzle, 165
Burrata, and Radicchio Pizzette with Black Olive Vinaigrette, 67–69, *68*
Chopped Salad with Flatbread and Labneh, 74
and Frisée Salad with Bacon, Poached Egg, and Whole-Wheat Croutons, *155*, 156
matchups of dressings and, 30
Poached Eggs with Asparagus and, with Lemon Vinaigrette,
Spring Herbs, and Parmesan Crostini, 53

Roasted Tomato Salad with *Fromage Chacun à Son Goût* and, 76, *77*

Asian Apple Pear Salad, Lamb Rib Chops with Cracked Wheat, Mint and, 190–91

Asian greens:
Buckwheat Soba Noodles with Sesame Dressing, Tofu and, 60
Chinese-Style Chicken Salad with Tangerines, *113*, 114–15

asparagus:
Grilled Baby Artichoke and, Salad with Shrimp and Saffron Aioli, *102*, 103–4
Poached Eggs with Arugula and, with Lemon Vinaigrette, Spring Herbs, and Parmesan Crostini, 53
Seared Salmon with Quinoa, Sorrel, Lemon Spinach and, *83*, 84–85
Smoked Salmon, and Watercress Salad with Sour Cream Dill Sauce, *96*, 97

avocado(s):
Caribbean Salad with Jerk Pork, 178
Chicken, and Mango Salad, 140, *141*
Cobb Salad, 123
Lime Dressing, Creamy, 49
Mexican Beach Ceviche with, 105
Salad, Seafood-Stuffed, 100, *101*

B

baby greens, 10
beet, pea, and fava bean leaves, 12
matchups of dressings and, 30
with Quince Vinaigrette, Artisanal Cheeses, and Charcuterie, 160–61, *161*

bacon:
Cobb Salad, 123
Frisée and Arugula Salad with Poached Egg, Whole-Wheat

Croutons and, *155*, 156

Maple Vinaigrette, 129

Mixed Greens with Farro, Dates, Walnuts, Pears, Parmesan and, *166*, 167

Balsamic Vinaigrette, 137
Fig, 171

Banh Mi Salad, Vietnamese Pork Meatball, 181–83, *182*

barley:
Fig, and Fennel Salad with Bûcheron, Speck, and Honey-Spice Walnuts, *170*, 171–72
Toasted, Long Bean, and Shiitake Mushroom Salad with Teriyaki Tofu, 46–47

basil:
Italian Chopped Salad, 168, *169*
Pesto, 72
Pesto Vinaigrette, 71, *73*

bean(s). *See also* chickpeas
Black, Tostada Salad with Jicama, Queso Fresco and, with Creamy Lime-Avocado Dressing and Chile Pepitas, 48–49
Kidney, Olive Bread Panzanella with Tomatoes, Lemon and, 57
White, and Baby Octopus Salad, 98

bean sprouts, in Korean Barbecue Beef Salad, 177

beef:
Argentine Grilled Steak and Vegetable Salad with Chimichurri Vinaigrette, 176
Bresaola and Arugula Salad with Parmesan Shavings and Lemon-Chive Drizzle, 165
Korean Barbecue, Salad, 177
Roast, with Red Leaf Lettuce, Red Onions, Radishes, and Horseradish Cream, 179
Steakhouse Salad, *174*, 175
Thai-Style Grilled, Salad, 180

beet(s):
Golden, Chicken and Orange Salad with, *130*, 131
leaves, baby, 10, 12
Roasted, 56

Roasted, and Blood Orange Salad
with Goat Cheese and Marcona
Almonds, *54*, 55–56
Roasted, Fennel, and Smoked
Whitefish Salad with
Horseradish Cream, 99
Trio of Grated Salads with Hearty
Greens and Pan-Seared
Sausages, 188, *189*
Belgian endive, 13
bento boxes, 23
Bibb lettuce, 12
bitter greens, matchups of dressings
and, 30
Black Beans, Tostada Salad with
Jicama, Queso Fresco and,
with Creamy Lime-Avocado
Dressing and Chile Pepitas,
48–49
blood orange. *See* orange(s)
blue cheese:
Baby Greens with Quince
Vinaigrette, Artisanal Cheeses,
and Charcuterie, 160–61, *161*
Cobb Salad, 123
Dressing, Creamy, 135
Smoked Turkey and Red Greens
Salad with Port Figs, Whole-
Wheat Croutons and, 146
Spicy Sriracha Buffalo Chicken
Salad, 134–35
Steakhouse Salad, *174, 175*
Boston lettuce, 12
bread. *See also* croutons; flatbread
Cornbread, Buttermilk, 159
Cornbread and Kale Salad, 157–59,
158
Croque Madame *Dans le Jardin*,
173
Crostini, Parmesan, 127, *127*
Naan Crisps, Garlic, *118*, 119
Olive, Panzanella with Tomatoes,
Kidney Beans, and Lemon, 57
pita, in Fattoush Salad with Lamb,
194, 195–96
and Red Mustard Salad with Roast
Chicken, 120–22, *121*
Bresaola and Arugula Salad with
Parmesan Shavings and
Lemon-Chive Drizzle, 165
Broccoli, Baby, Sautéed Duck
Breast Salad with Kumquats,
Dried Cherries, Five-Spice
Vinaigrette and, 150, *151*

brown rice:
Grape Leaf Salad, 58, *59*
pad thai noodles, in Thai Grilled
Beef Salad, 180
Brussels Sprout, Roasted Acorn
Squash and, Salad with Quinoa,
Pepitas, and Pomegranates, *40*,
41–42
Bûcheron, Fig, Fennel, and Barley
Salad with Speck, Honey-Spice
Walnuts and, *170*, 171–72
Buckwheat Soba Noodles with
Sesame Dressing, Tofu, and
Asian Greens, 60
Buffalo Chicken Salad, Spicy
Sriracha, with Creamy Blue
Cheese Dressing, 134–35
Burrata, Arugula, and Radicchio
Pizzette with Black Olive
Vinaigrette, 67–69, *68*
butter lettuce, 13
matchups of dressings and, 30
buttermilk:
Cornbread, 159
Dressing, 157–59, *158*
Fried Chicken and Green Salad
with Maple-Bacon Vinaigrette,
128–29

C

cabbage, 13
Indonesian Slaw with Pineapple,
Chicken, and Spicy Peanut
Dressing, 116
Jeanne's Jar Chopped Salad, *124*,
125
matchups of dressings and, 30
napa, in Chinese-Style Chicken
Salad with Tangerines, *113*,
114–15
napa, in Korean Barbecue Beef
Salad, 177
Caesar Salad with Grilled Chicken
and Parmesan Crostini, 126–27
Caribbean Salad with Jerk Pork, 178
carrot(s):
Lentil and Smoked Turkey Salad
with Roasted Parsnips
and, on Peppery Greens,
144–45
Moroccan-Spiced Roasted
Cauliflower and, Salad with
Chickpeas and Couscous,
44–45

Trio of Grated Salads with Hearty
Greens and Pan-Seared
Sausages, 188, *189*
cashews, 28
Kohlrabi and Black Quinoa Salad
with Coconut and, 61
Cauliflower, Moroccan-Spiced
Roasted Carrot and, Salad
with Chickpeas and Couscous,
44–45
celery root, in Trio of Grated Salads
with Hearty Greens and Pan-
Seared Sausages, 188, *189*
Ceviche, Mexican Beach, with
Avocado, 105
Charcuterie, Baby Greens with
Quince Vinaigrette, Artisanal
Cheeses and, 160–61, *161*
cheddar cheese, in Kale and
Cornbread Salad, 157–59, *158*
cheese(s). *See also* blue cheese; feta
cheese; goat cheese; mozzarella
cheese; Parmesan cheese
Artisanal, Baby Greens
with Quince Vinaigrette,
Charcuterie and, 160–61, *161*
Bûcheron, Fig, Fennel, and Barley
Salad with Speck, Honey-Spice
Walnuts and, *170*, 171–72
Burrata, Arugula, and Radicchio
Pizzette with Black Olive
Vinaigrette, 67–69, *68*
cheddar, in Kale and Cornbread
Salad, 157–59, *158*
Gruyère, in Croque Madame *Dans
le Jardin*, 173
Haloumi, Grilled, Freekeh Salad
with Apricots, Zucchini and,
78, *79*
Italian, in Italian Chopped Salad,
168, *169*
Labneh, Chopped Salad with
Flatbread and, 74
Manchego, in Spanish
Chopped Salad with Migas,
162, 163
Queso Fresco, Tostada Salad
with Black Beans, Jicama and,
with Creamy Lime-Avocado
Dressing and Chile Pepitas,
48–49
Roasted Tomato Salad with
Arugula and *Fromage Chacun à
Son Goût*, 76, *77*

Cherries, Dried, Sautéed Duck Breast Salad with Kumquats, Baby Broccoli, Five-Spice Vinaigrette and, 150, *151*

chervil, 10, 14

chicken:
    Avocado, and Mango Salad, 140, *141*
    Breasts, Roast, 119
    Buffalo, Salad, Spicy Sriracha, with Creamy Blue Cheese Dressing, 134–35
    Buttermilk Fried, and Green Salad with Maple-Bacon Vinaigrette, 128–29
    Cobb Salad, 123
    Grilled, Caesar Salad with Parmesan Crostini and, 126–27
    Grilled, Salad, Oregon Summer, 132, *133*
    Indonesian Slaw with Pineapple, Spicy Peanut Dressing and, 116
    Jeanne's Jar Chopped Salad, *124*, 125
    and Orange Salad with Golden Beets, *130*, 131
    Roast, Red Mustard and Bread Salad with, 120–22, *121*
    Roast, Simple, with Fingerling Potatoes, 143
    Roasted Balsamic, and Green Bean Salad with Goat Cheese, *136*, 137
    Salad, Curried, on Baby Spinach with Mango Chutney Dressing and Garlic Naan Crisps, 117–19, *118*
    Salad, Thai Larb, 138–39
    Salad Waldorf-Style, 142
    Salad with Tangerines, Chinese-Style, *113*, 114–15

chickpeas (garbanzo beans):
    Italian Chopped Salad, 168, *169*
    Moroccan-Spiced Roasted Cauliflower and Carrot Salad with Couscous and, 44–45

chickweed, 18

Chimichurri Vinaigrette, 176

Chinese New Year Raw Fish "Tossed" Salad, Singapore-Style, *88*, 89–90

Chinese-Style Chicken Salad with Tangerines, *113*, 114–15

Chive-Lemon Drizzle, 165

Chocolate Cream Pie, *198*, 199

chopped salads:
    with Flatbread and Labneh, 74
    Italian, 168, *169*
    Jeanne's Jar, *124*, 125
    Spanish, with Migas, *162*, 163

chorizo:
    Baby Greens with Quince Vinaigrette, Artisanal Cheeses, and Charcuterie, 160–61, *161*
    Spanish Chopped Salad with Migas, *162*, 163

Chutney, Mango, Dressing, 117

citrus supremes, 131

Cobb Salad, 123

Coconut, Kohlrabi and Black Quinoa Salad with Cashews and, 61

condiments:
    Lemons, Preserved, 87
    Romesco Sauce, 185
    Saffron Aioli, *102*, 104
    Spicy Mayo, 181

corn:
    and Ham Salad, Summertime, 164
    Oakleaf Lettuce with Grilled Pork, Nectarines and, with Honey-Marjoram Vinaigrette, 186–87

cornbread:
    Buttermilk, 159
    and Kale Salad, 157–59, *158*

Couscous, Moroccan-Spiced Roasted Cauliflower and Carrot Salad with Chickpeas and, 44–45

crabmeat, in Seafood-Stuffed Avocado Salad, 100, *101*

Cracked Wheat, Lamb Rib Chops with Mint, Asian Apple Pear Salad and, 190–91

crisphead lettuce, 13

Croque Madame *Dans le Jardin*, 173

Crostini, Parmesan, 127, *127*

Croutons, 70
    Migas, Spanish Chopped Salad with, *162*, 163
    Whole-Wheat, 146

CSA (Community Sustainable Agriculture), 24

cucumbers, Persian, 66
    Chopped Salad with Flatbread and Labneh, 74
    Greek Salad, 52
    Green Goddess Salad, 64–66, *65*

curly endive, 10, 14

Curried Chicken Salad on Baby Spinach with Mango Chutney Dressing and Garlic Naan Crisps, 117–19, *118*

D

dandelion, 18

Dates, Mixed Greens with Farro, Bacon, Walnuts, Pears, Parmesan and, *166*, 167

dessert: Chocolate Cream Pie, *198*, 199

Dill Sour Cream Sauce, *96*, 97

dressings, 28, 29. *See also* vinaigrettes
    Blue Cheese, Creamy, 135
    Buttermilk, 157–59, *158*
    Caesar, 126
    Garlic-Mint Yogurt, 197
    Green Goddess, 66
    health benefits of, 145
    Horseradish Cream, 99
    Jerk, 178
    leftover, combining, 31
    Lemon, Mediterranean, 196
    Lemon-Chive Drizzle, 165
    Lime-Avocado, Creamy, 49
    Mango Chutney, 117
    matchups of greens and, 30–31
    Moroccan-Spiced, 45
    Peanut, Spicy, 116
    Sesame, 60
    Sour Cream Dill Sauce, *96*, 97
    Spicy Mayo, 181
    Thai, 139

duck:
    Breast, Sautéed, Salad with Kumquats, Baby Broccoli, Dried Cherries, and Five-Spice Vinaigrette, 150, *151*
    Breast, Smoked, Salad with Haricots Verts, Apricots, and Pistachios, 147
    Confit Salad with Fingerlings and Frisée, 148

E

egg(s):
    Croque Madame *Dans le Jardin*, 173
    Fried, Wilted Swiss Chard "Salad" with Caramelized Onions, Croutons and, 70

Hardboiled, 97

hardboiled, in Cobb Salad, 123

hardboiled, in Green Goddess
    Salad, 64–66, 65

Poached, Frisée and Arugula Salad
    with Bacon, Whole-Wheat
    Croutons and, 155, 156

Poached, with Asparagus
    and Arugula with Lemon
    Vinaigrette, Spring Herbs, and
    Parmesan Crostini, 53

Eggplant, Grilled, with Heirloom
    Tomatoes, Fresh Mozzarella,
    and Pesto Vinaigrette, 71–72, 73

escarole, 14

F

farro:

    Kale Salad with Parmesan, Pine
        Nuts, Currants and, 43

    Mixed Greens with Bacon, Dates,
        Walnuts, Pears, Parmesan and,
        166, 167

    Fattoush Salad with Lamb, 194,
        195–96

fava bean leaves, 12

fennel:

    Fig, and Barley Salad with
        Bûcheron, Speck, and Honey-
        Spice Walnuts, 170, 171–72

    Italian Chopped Salad, 168, 169

    Roasted Beet, and Smoked
        Whitefish Salad with
        Horseradish Cream, 99

feta cheese:

    Greek Salad, 52

    Green Goddess Salad, 64–66, 65

    Jeanne's Jar Chopped Salad, 124,
        125

    Olive Bread Panzanella with
        Tomatoes, Kidney Beans, and
        Lemon, 57

fig(s):

    Balsamic Vinaigrette, 171

    Fennel, and Barley Salad with
        Bûcheron, Speck, and Honey-
        Spice Walnuts, 170, 171–72

    Port, Smoked Turkey and Red
        Greens Salad with Blue Cheese,
        Whole-Wheat Croutons and,
        146

Fish, Raw, "Tossed" Salad,
    Singapore-Style Chinese New
    Year, 88, 89–90

Five-Spice Vinaigrette, 150

flatbread:

    Burrata, Arugula, and Radicchio
        Pizzette with Black Olive
        Vinaigrette, 67–69, 68

    Chopped Salad with Labneh and,
        74

    Dough, 69

foraging for salad, 18–19

Freekeh Salad with Apricots, Grilled
    Haloumi, and Zucchini, 78, 79

frisée, 10, 14, 21

    and Arugula Salad with Bacon,
        Poached Egg, and Whole-
        Wheat Croutons, 155, 156

    Duck Confit Salad with
        Fingerlings and, 148

    Salad with Goat Cheese and
        Roasted Grapes, 75

G

garbanzo beans. See chickpeas

garlic:

    Mint Yogurt Dressing, 197

    Naan Crisps, 118, 119

garnishes:

    Chile Pepitas, 48

    Honey-Spice Glazed Walnuts,
        172, 172

goat cheese:

    Baby Greens with Quince
        Vinaigrette and Artisanal
        Cheeses and Charcuterie,
        160–61, 161

    Frisée Salad with Roasted Grapes
        and, 75

    Roasted Balsamic Chicken and
        Green Bean Salad with, 136, 137

    Roasted Beet and Blood Orange
        Salad with Marcona Almonds
        and, 54, 55–56

    Toasts, 51

grapefruit:

    Caribbean Salad with Jerk Pork,
        178

    supremes, 131

Grape Leaf Brown Rice Salad,
    58, 59

Grapes, Roasted, Frisée Salad with
    Goat Cheese and, 75

Grated Salads, Trio of, with Hearty
    Greens and Pan-Seared
    Sausages, 188, 189

Greek Salad, 52

green bean(s). See also haricots verts

    Long Bean, Toasted Barley, and
        Shiitake Mushroom Salad with
        Teriyaki Tofu, 46–47

    and Roasted Balsamic Chicken
        Salad with Goat Cheese, 136,
        137

green goddess:

    Dressing, 66

    Salad, 64–66, 65

greens. See salad greens

green salad bowl lettuce, 10, 14

grilled:

    Artichoke and Asparagus Salad
        with Shrimp, 102, 103–4

    Beef Salad, Korean Barbecue, 177

    Beef Salad, Thai-Style, 180

    Chicken, Caesar Salad with
        Parmesan Crostini and, 126–27

    Chicken Salad, Oregon Summer,
        132, 133

    Eggplant with Heirloom
        Tomatoes, Fresh Mozzarella,
        and Pesto Vinaigrette, 71–72, 73

    Kale with Lamb and Garlic-Mint
        Yogurt Dressing, 197

    Lamb, Fattoush Salad with, 194,
        195–96

    Lamb Kebabs, 194, 196

    Pork, Oakleaf Lettuce with Corn,
        Nectarines and, with Honey-
        Marjoram Vinaigrette, 186–87

    Pork and Green Onions with
        Romesco Sauce, Greens, and
        Sherry Vinaigrette, 184–85

    Shrimp and Peppers, Spinach
        Salad with, 106, 107

    Steak and Vegetable Salad with
        Chimichurri Vinaigrette,
        Argentine, 176

growing greens, 24–25

Gruyère cheese, in Croque Madame
    Dans le Jardin, 173

H

Haloumi, Grilled, Freekeh Salad
    with Apricots, Zucchini and,
    78, 79

ham:

    and Corn Salad, Summertime, 164

    Croque Madame Dans le Jardin,
        173

    Kale and Cornbread Salad, 157–59,
        158

haricots verts:
    Green Goddess Salad, 64–66, *65*
    Smoked Duck Breast Salad with
        Apricots, Pistachios and, 147
herb(s), 14
    Mustard Version of Coffee-Mug
        Mayo, 183
    Za'atar, 74
honey:
    Marjoram Vinaigrette, 187
    Spice Glazed Walnuts, 172, *172*
Horseradish Cream, 99

I

iceberg lettuce, 13
Indonesian Slaw with Pineapple,
    Chicken, and Spicy Peanut
    Dressing, 116
ingredients. *See also* salad greens
    guidelines for incorporation of, 33
    seasonal, 22
Italian Chopped Salad, 168, *169*

J

Jeanne's Jar Chopped Salad, *124*, 125
Jerk Pork, Caribbean Salad with, 178
Jicama, Tostada Salad with Black
    Beans, Queso Fresco and,
    with Creamy Lime-Avocado
    Dressing and Chile Pepitas,
    48–49

K

kale, 15
    and Cornbread Salad, 157–59, *158*
    Grilled, with Lamb and Garlic-
        Mint Yogurt Dressing, 197
    matchups of dressings and, 30
    Salad with Wheat Berries,
        Parmesan, Pine Nuts, and
        Currants, 43
Kidney Beans, Olive Bread
    Panzanella with Tomatoes,
    Lemon and, 57
Kohlrabi and Black Quinoa Salad
    with Coconut and Cashews, 61
Korean Barbecue Beef Salad, 177
Kumquats, Sautéed Duck Breast
    Salad with Baby Broccoli,
    Dried Cherries, Five-Spice
    Vinaigrette and, 150, *151*

L

Labneh, Chopped Salad with

Flatbread and, 74
lamb:
    Fattoush Salad with, *194*, 195–96
    Grilled Kale with, and Garlic-Mint
        Yogurt Dressing, 197
    Rib Chops with Cracked Wheat,
        Mint, and Asian Apple Pear
        Salad, 190–91
lamb's quarters, 19
lemon(s):
    Chive Drizzle, 165
    Dressing, Mediterranean, 196
    Preserved, 87
    Vinaigrette, 85
Lentil and Smoked Turkey Salad
    with Roasted Carrots and
    Parsnips on Peppery Greens,
    144–45
lettuces. *See* salad greens
lime:
    Ancho Vinaigrette, 39
    Avocado Dressing, Creamy, 49
limestone lettuce, 12
little gem lettuce, 15
Lobster Salad with Watermelon,
    Yellow Tomato, Mâche, and
    Mint, 92, *93*
Long Bean, Toasted Barley, and
    Shiitake Mushroom Salad with
    Teriyaki Tofu, 46–47

M

mâche, 15
    Lobster Salad with Watermelon,
        Yellow Tomato, Mint and, 92, *93*
make-ahead salads, 26
Manchego cheese, in Spanish
    Chopped Salad with Migas,
    162, 163
mango:
    Caribbean Salad with Jerk Pork,
        178
    Chicken, and Avocado Salad, 140,
        141
    Chutney Dressing, 117
Maple-Bacon Vinaigrette, 129
Marjoram-Honey Vinaigrette, 187
mayo:
    Coffee-Mug, 183
    Spicy, 181
measuring greens, 21
Meatball, Pork, Vietnamese Banh Mi
    Salad, 181–83, *182*
Mediterranean Lemon Dressing, 196

mesclun, 10, 11
Mexican Beach Ceviche with
    Avocado, 105
Migas, Spanish Chopped Salad with,
    162, 163
miner's lettuce, 19
mint:
    Garlic Yogurt Dressing, 197
    Lamb Rib Chops with Cracked
        Wheat, Asian Apple Pear Salad
        and, 190–91
    Lobster Salad with Watermelon,
        Yellow Tomato, Mâche and,
        92, *93*
    Orecchiette and Pea Salad with
        Perlini Mozzarella and, *62*, 63
mixed greens, 10
    with Farro, Bacon, Dates, Walnuts,
        Pears, and Parmesan, *166*, 167
    matchups of dressings and, 30
mizuna, 10, 15
Moroccan-Spiced Roasted
    Cauliflower and Carrot Salad
    with Chickpeas and Couscous,
    44–45
mozzarella cheese:
    Grilled Eggplant with Heirloom
        Tomatoes, Pesto Vinaigrette
        and, 71–72, *73*
    Perlini, Orecchiette and Pea Salad
        with Mint and, *62*, 63
mushroom:
    Shiitake, Toasted Barley, and Long
        Bean Salad with Teriyaki Tofu,
        46–47
    Wild, Salad, Warm, with Goat
        Cheese Toasts, 50–51
mustard:
    Herb Version of Coffee-Mug Mayo,
        183
    Shallot Vinaigrette, 145

N

Naan Crisps, Garlic, *118*, 119
napa cabbage. *See* cabbage
Nectarines, Oakleaf Lettuce with
    Grilled Pork, Corn and, with
    Honey-Marjoram Vinaigrette,
    186–87
nettles, 19
noodles. *See also* pasta
    brown rice pad thai, in Thai
        Grilled Beef Salad, 180
    Buckwheat Soba, with Sesame

Dressing, Tofu, and Asian
Greens, 60
rice stick, in Chinese-Style
Chicken Salad with Tangerines,
113, 114–15
nuts, 28

O

oakleaf lettuce, 15
with Grilled Pork, Corn, and
Nectarines with Honey-
Marjoram Vinaigrette, 186–87
Octopus, Baby, and White Bean
Salad, 98
oils, 28
olive(s):
Black, Vinaigrette, 67–69, *68*
Bread Panzanella with Tomatoes,
Kidney Beans, and Lemon, 57
Italian Chopped Salad, 168, *169*
kalamata, in Greek Salad, 52
onions:
Caramelized, Wilted Swiss Chard
"Salad" with Croutons, Fried
Eggs and, 70
Green, Grilled Pork and, with
Romesco Sauce, Greens, and
Sherry Vinaigrette, 184–85
orange(s):
Blood, and Roasted Beet Salad
with Goat Cheese and Marcona
Almonds, *54*, 55
Blood, Sherry Vinaigrette, 55
Caribbean Salad with Jerk Pork,
178
and Chicken Salad with Golden
Beets, *130*, 131
Orecchiette and Pea Salad with
Perlini Mozzarella and Mint,
62, 63
Oregano Vinaigrette, 52
Oregon Summer Grilled Chicken
Salad, 132, *133*
orzo pasta, in Paella Salad, 108, *109*

P

packing salad to go, 23
Paella Salad, 108, *109*
pantry, 28–29
Panzanella, Olive Bread, with
Tomatoes, Kidney Beans, and
Lemon, 57
Parmesan cheese:
Crostini, 127, *127*

Mixed Greens with Farro, Bacon,
Dates, Walnuts, Pears and,
166, 167
Shavings, Bresaola and Arugula
Salad with Lemon-Chive
Drizzle and, 165
parsley, 10, 14
White Anchovy, and Potato Salad,
91
Parsnips, Lentil and Smoked Turkey
Salad with Roasted Carrots and,
on Peppery Greens, 144–45
party salads, 192–93
pasta. *See also* noodles
Orecchiette and Pea Salad with
Perlini Mozzarella and Mint,
62, 63
orzo, in Paella Salad, 108, *109*
pea:
leaves, baby, 12
and Orecchiette Salad with Perlini
Mozzarella and Mint, *62*, 63
Peanut Dressing, Spicy, 116
Pears, Mixed Greens with Farro,
Bacon, Dates, Walnuts,
Parmesan and, *166*, 167
pecans, 28
pepitas:
Chile, 48
Roasted Acorn Squash and
Brussels Sprout Salad with
Quinoa, Pomegranates and, 40,
41–42
pepper(s). *See also* piquillo peppers
Argentine Grilled Steak and
Vegetable Salad with
Chimichurri Vinaigrette, 176
Red, Version of Coffee-Mug Mayo,
183
Spinach Salad with Grilled Shrimp
and, *100*, 107
peppery greens, 10–11
matchups of dressings and, 31
Pesto, 72
Vinaigrette, 71, *73*
Pickled Vegetables, 181
Pie, Chocolate Cream, *198*, 199
Pineapple, Indonesian Slaw with
Chicken, Spicy Peanut Dressing
and, 116
piquillo peppers:
Romesco Sauce, 185
Sardine-Stuffed, with Greens and
Croutons, 86–87

pistachios, 28
Smoked Duck Breast Salad with
Haricots Verts, Apricots and,
147
pita bread, in Fattoush Salad with
Lamb, *194*, 195–96
Pizzette, Burrata, Arugula, and
Radicchio, with Black Olive
Vinaigrette, 67–69, *68*
Pomegranates, Roasted Acorn
Squash and Brussels Sprout
Salad with Quinoa, Pepitas and,
40, 41–42
pork:
Grilled, and Green Onions with
Romesco Sauce, Greens,
and Sherry Vinaigrette,
184–85
Grilled, Oakleaf Lettuce with
Corn, Nectarines and, with
Honey-Marjoram Vinaigrette,
186–87
Jerk, Caribbean Salad with,
178
Meatball Banh Mi Salad,
Vietnamese, 181–83, *182*
Port Figs, Smoked Turkey and Red
Greens Salad with Blue Cheese,
Whole-Wheat Croutons and,
146
potato(es):
Fingerling, Duck Confit Salad with
Frisée and, 148
Fingerling, Simple Roast Chicken
with, 143
Steakhouse Salad, *174*, 175
White Anchovy, and Parsley
Salad, 91
prosciutto:
Baby Greens with Quince
Vinaigrette, Artisanal Cheeses,
and Charcuterie, 160–61, *161*
Jeanne's Jar Chopped Salad, *124*,
125
puntarelle, 16
purslane, 16

Q

Queso Fresco, Tostada Salad with
Black Beans, Jicama and,
with Creamy Lime-Avocado
Dressing and Chile Pepitas,
48–49
Quince Vinaigrette, 161

quinoa:
    Black, and Kohlrabi Salad with
        Coconut and Cashews, 61
    Roasted Acorn Squash and
        Brussels Sprout Salad with
        Pepitas, Pomegranates and, *40*,
        41–42
    Seared Salmon with Asparagus,
        Sorrel, Lemon Spinach and, *83*,
        84–85

R
radicchio, 10, 16
    Burrata, and Arugula Pizzette
        with Black Olive Vinaigrette,
        67–69, *68*
    Italian Chopped Salad, 168, *169*
red mustard, 10, 16
    and Bread Salad with Roast
        Chicken, 120–22, *121*
red salad bowl lettuce, 10, 14
red wine vinegar, house-made, 149
Rice, Brown, Grape Leaf Salad,
    58, *59*
rice noodles:
    brown rice pad thai, in Thai
        Grilled Beef Salad, 180
    rice sticks, in Chinese-Style
        Chicken Salad with Tangerines,
        113, 114–15
romaine, 10, 17, 21
    matchups of dressings and, 30
Romesco Sauce, 185

S
Saffron Aioli, *102*, 104
Salade Lyonnaise (Frisée and
    Arugula Salad with Bacon,
    Poached Egg, and Whole-
    Wheat Croutons), *155*, 156
Salade Niçoise un Peu Classique,
    94–95
salad greens, 9–21
    foraging for, 18–19
    glossary of, 12–17
    growing, 24–25
    lettuce, salads without, 27
    measuring, 21
    three blends of, 10–11
    washing and storing, 20–21
salad spinners, 20–21
salami:
    Baby Greens with Quince
        Vinaigrette, Artisanal

Cheeses, Charcuterie, 160–61,
    161
Italian Chopped Salad, 168, *169*
salmon:
    Seared, with Quinoa, Asparagus,
        Sorrel, and Lemon Spinach, *83*,
        84–85
    Smoked, Asparagus, and
        Watercress Salad with Sour
        Cream Dill Sauce, *96*, 97
salt, 29
Sardine-Stuffed Piquillo Peppers
    with Lemony Greens and
    Whole-Wheat Croutons, 86–87
sausages. *See also* chorizo
    Pan-Seared, Trio of Grated Salads
        with Hearty Greens and, 188,
        189
scallops, in Mexican Beach Ceviche
    with Avocado, 105
Seafood-Stuffed Avocado Salad,
    100, *101*
seasonal ingredients, 22
Sesame Dressing, 60
Shallot-Mustard Vinaigrette, 145
sherry:
    Blood Orange Vinaigrette, 55
    Vinaigrette, 184
Shiitake Mushroom, Toasted Barley,
    and Long Bean Salad with
    Teriyaki Tofu, 46–47
shrimp:
    Grilled Baby Artichoke and
        Asparagus Salad with Saffron
        Aioli and, *102*, 103–4
    Paella Salad, 108, *109*
    Seafood-Stuffed Avocado Salad,
        100, *101*
    Spinach Salad with Grilled
        Peppers and, *106*, 107
Singapore-Style Chinese New Year
    Raw Fish "Tossed" Salad, *88*,
    89–90
Slaw, Indonesian, with Pineapple,
    Chicken, and Spicy Peanut
    Dressing, 116
Soba Noodles, Buckwheat, with
    Sesame Dressing, Tofu, and
    Asian Greens, 60
sorrel, 14
    Seared Salmon with Quinoa,
        Asparagus, Lemon Spinach and,
        83, 84–85
sour cream:

Dill Sauce, *96*, 97
Horseradish Cream, 99
Spanish Chopped Salad with Migas,
    162, 163
Speck, Fig, Fennel, and Barley Salad
    with Bûcheron, Honey-Spice
    Walnuts and, *170*, 171–72
Spicy Mayo, 181
Spicy Peanut Dressing, 116
Spicy Sriracha Buffalo Chicken
    Salad with Creamy Blue Cheese
    Dressing, 134–35
spinach, 10, 17
    Baby, Curried Chicken Salad on,
        with Mango Chutney Dressing
        and Garlic Naan Crisps, 117–19,
        118
    Lemon, Seared Salmon with
        Quinoa, Asparagus, Sorrel and,
        83, 84–85
    matchups of dressings and, 31
    Salad with Grilled Shrimp and
        Peppers, *106*, 107
    Sriracha Buffalo Chicken Salad,
        Spicy, with Creamy Blue
        Cheese Dressing, 134–35
steak:
    Grilled Vegetable and, Salad
        with Chimichurri Vinaigrette,
        Argentine, 176
    Steakhouse Salad, *174*, 175
Summertime Corn and Ham Salad,
    164
Swiss chard, 10, 17
    Wilted, "Salad" with Caramelized
        Onions, Croutons, and Fried
        Eggs, 70

T
tahini, in Mediterranean Lemon
    Dressing, 196
Tangerines, Chinese-Style Chicken
    Salad with, *113*, 114–15
tatsoi, 10, 17
Teriyaki Tofu Cubes, Baked, 47
Thai:
    Dressing, 139
    Grilled Beef Salad, 180
    Larb Chicken Salad, 138–39
tilapia, in Mexican Beach Ceviche
    with Avocado, 105
timeline for salad preparation,
    26–27
Toasts, Goat Cheese, 51

tofu:
  Buckwheat Soba Noodles with
    Sesame Dressing, Asian Greens
    and, 60
  Cubes, Baked Teriyaki, 47
tomato(es):
  Chopped Salad with Flatbread and
    Labneh, 74
  Heirloom, Grilled Eggplant
    with Fresh Mozzarella, Pesto
    Vinaigrette and, 71–72, 73
  Olive Bread Panzanella with
    Kidney Beans, Lemon and, 57
  Roasted, Salad with Arugula and
    Fromage Chacun à Son Goût,
    76, 77
  Yellow, Lobster Salad with
    Watermelon, Mâche, Mint and,
    92, 93
  Tostada Salad with Black Beans,
    Jicama, and Queso Fresco with
    Creamy Lime-Avocado Dressing
    and Chile Pepitas, 48–49
  Trio of Grated Salads with Hearty
    Greens and Pan-Seared
    Sausages, 188, 189
tuna, in *Salade Niçoise un Peu
    Classique*, 94–95
turkey, smoked:
  and Lentil Salad with Roasted
    Carrots and Parsnips on
    Peppery Greens, 144–45
  and Red Greens Salad with Port
    Figs, Blue Cheese, and Whole-
    Wheat Croutons, 146

U
umami, 51

V
Vietnamese Pork Meatball Banh Mi
    Salad, 181–83, 182
vinaigrettes, 28. *See also* dressings
  Anchovy, 95
  Balsamic, 137
  Black Olive, 67–69, 68
  Blood Orange–Sherry, 55
  Chimichurri, 176
  creative uses for, 32
  Fig Balsamic, 171
  Five-Spice, 150
  Honey-Marjoram, 187
  leftover, combining, 31
  Lemon, 85
  Lime-Ancho, 39
  Maple-Bacon, 129
  matchups of greens and, 30–31
  Mustard-Shallot, 145
  Oregano, 52
  Pesto, 71, 73
  Quince, 161
  Sherry, 184
vinegar, 29
  red wine, house-made, 149

W
Waldorf-Style Chicken Salad, 142
walnuts, 28
  Honey-Spice Glazed, 172, 172
  Mixed Greens with Farro, Bacon,
    Dates, Pears, Parmesan and,
    166, 167
washing greens, 20–21
watercress, 17
  Smoked Salmon, and Asparagus
    Salad with Sour Cream Dill
    Sauce, 96, 97

Watermelon, Lobster Salad with
    Yellow Tomato, Mâche, Mint
    and, 92, 93
Wheat Berries, Kale Salad with
    Parmesan, Pine Nuts, Currants
    and, 43
White Bean and Baby Octopus
    Salad, 98
Whitefish, Smoked, Fennel, and
    Roasted Beet Salad with
    Horseradish Cream, 99
Whole-Wheat Croutons, 146
Wild Rice and Winter Greens Salad
    with Grilled Yams and Lime-
    Ancho Vinaigrette, 37, 38–39
Winter Greens and Wild Rice Salad
    with Grilled Yams and Lime-
    Ancho Vinaigrette, 37, 38–39
Wonton Strips, Fried, 90
wood sorrel, 19

Y
Yams, Grilled, Winter Greens and
    Wild Rice Salad with Lime-
    Ancho Vinaigrette and, 37,
    38–39
Yogurt Dressing, Garlic-Mint, 197

Z
Za'atar, 74
zucchini:
  Argentine Grilled Steak and
    Vegetable Salad with
    Chimichurri Vinaigrette, 176
  Freekeh Salad with Apricots,
    Grilled Haloumi and, 78, 79